…roadcaster; her best-
… *A Far Country* and …

Columba Cary-Elwes is a monk of the Order of St Benedict, Ampleforth.

Bishop Victor Guazzelli is Bishop in East London, within the Archdiocese of Westminster.

John Harriott is a regular columnist for *The Tablet*, with a particular interest in the state of the Church in England.

Douglas Brown, an Anglican, is a freelance journalist and a former Religious Affairs Correspondent of the BBC.

Chris Cviic writes on religious affairs for *The Economist* and is editor of Chatham House's monthly magazine *The World Today*.

Clifford Longley is Religious Affairs Correspondent of *The Times*.

Hugo Young was taught by Basil Hume at Ampleforth, and is now a political columnist on *The Guardian*.

Tony Castle, a freelance writer and editor and former editor of *Christian Celebration*, is the author of *Tomorrow's People* and *Let's Celebrate*; he has compiled *Quotes and Anecdotes for Preachers and Teachers; Through the Year with Pope John Paul II* and *The Perfection of Love*.

BASIL HUME

A PORTRAIT

edited by
TONY CASTLE

Collins
FOUNT PAPERBACKS

First published in Great Britain in 1986
by William Collins Sons & Co. Ltd, London
Published by Fount Paperbacks, London, in 1987

Made and printed in Great Britain by
William Collins Sons & Co. Ltd, Glasgow

CONTENTS

ILLUSTRATIONS

All other photographs are from the Andes Press Agency

INTRODUCTION

Early in the winter of 1975 history's first consultative process in the Archdiocese of Westminster, to find a successor to John Carmel Heenan, had thrown up ninety names! Every possible church viewpoint and lobby was represented. In the Catholic press of 28th November Dom Benet Innes OSB appealed for an end to the lobbying and the labels, and uttered a cry from the heart, 'Give us a man of God'.

The new direction that the Catholic Church in England and Wales was about to take was hinted at on Friday, 13th February 1976, when *The Universe* broke the news that Bishop Derek Worlock would be the new Archbishop of Liverpool. One week later the same newspaper carried a more astonishing announcement:

> The surprise appointment of the Rt Rev. George Basil Hume OSB, Abbot of Ampleforth, as the ninth Archbishop of Westminster, puts an emphasis on spiritual values at a time when many Catholics are sick and tired of debate and argument.

On Thursday, 25th March, George Basil Hume OSB was ordained bishop by the Apostolic Delegate, Archbishop Heim, and installed as Archbishop of Westminster; two months later, on 24th May, he was created cardinal.

Cardinal Hume was, at first, ill at ease with the idea that we intended to mark his tenth anniversary with a tribute to his life and work. His letter to me on the subject revealed not a little of his spirituality, and a touch of the schoolmaster:

> I hope that the tenth year will be ignored while I struggle on to be better in my job in the eleventh.

The theme of struggling on, a pilgrim in search of God, gave the titles to his two books, *Searching for God* and *To be a Pilgrim*, both of which established themselves as modern spiritual classics.

That the struggle and the pilgrimage have been essentially an inward journey is evident from the 'presence' about Basil Hume, which people of all walks of life and every conceivable background recognize. It is not, as with most public figures, a presence that is projected onto him or wrapped around him, but emanates from within. Here, people instinctively feel, is a man who has searched and found. One illuminating passage from *Searching for God* casts light upon the 'how' of it:

> The art of being a monk is to know how to be in the desert and how to be in the market-place . . . By the desert I mean withdrawal from activity and people to meet God. By the market-place I mean involvement in pastoral situations of one kind or another (p. 33).

Basil Hume's effective involvement in pastoral situations, expertly portrayed by the writers in this book, is clearly a product of his love of meeting God in the desert. This found perfect expression in his final public address to the Ampleforth community, on Sunday, 22nd February 1976, when he said, 'Whatever I achieve will be God's achievement, not mine.'

I am grateful to the eight distinguished writers who accepted with enthusiasm my invitation to contribute to this book. I alone know what an immense strain, given the short period of time available to them, that the acceptance placed upon most of them in the midst of their busy work schedules. We have all considered it a labour of love, and are thankful that Dom Benet Innes' prayer in November 1975 has been so wonderfully answered.

October 1985 TONY CASTLE

1

The Early Years

When Marie Elisabeth Hume was expecting her third child, she already had two daughters, a matter of some regret within the French family from which she sprang, which regarded boys with more favour. Her confessor, Father Johnson, at the Holy Name Church in Newcastle, tried to look on the bright side: 'This time let's all pray the baby will be a boy, and that he'll grow up to be a priest', he encouraged her.

The baby, born on 2nd March 1923 and christened George Haliburton Hume, went on to become not only a priest but a Cardinal Archbishop, thus doubtless exceeding his mother's and Father Johnson's hopes. These hopes were not shared, however, by the baby's Protestant father, William Errington Hume, to whom his elder son's eventual decision to enter a monastery would come as a grave disappointment.

But all that lay in the future and, in any case, did not essentially disrupt the harmony of an exceptionally happy and close-knit family – so happy and close-knit, in fact, that one cleric laughingly accused Marie of doing a disservice to the Church by making 'mixed marriages' look far too easy.

George Haliburton Hume (Haliburton was his great-grandmother's maiden name) was born into a family with a rich mix of ancestral talents and temperaments. On his Scots-English (Northumbrian) father's side, were a number of distinguished medical men and a sprinkling of Anglican divines; while in his French mother's family, high-ranking army officers rubbed shoulders with industrial entrepreneurs. George's father (the son of another George Haliburton Hume, the historian of the Newcastle Infirmary) was to become one of Newcastle's most distinguished medical men, a world authority on heart-diseases. William Hume studied medicine at Cambridge and at the London Hospital (where he was an assistant to Sir Bertrand Dawson, later Lord Dawson of Penn), before returning to Newcastle to become senior House Physician at the Infirmary. He appears to have made his mark fairly rapidly, introducing modern scientific techniques to the Infirmary, and becoming the first man in Newcastle to make use of the new electro-cardiograph.

When war broke out in 1914, William joined the RAMC and was sent to France, where for a short time he worked in a Casualty Clearing Station. Soon, however, his former chief, Dawson, caught up with him and brought him to work in the base hospitals around Boulogne. Here Hume found himself organizing centres for the investigation and treatment of soldiers with cardiac complaints, and, with Dawson and another Newcastle doctor, S. P. Bedson, studying the causes of the spirochaetal jaundice which was currently ravaging the troops. Before long he was appointed Consulting Physician to the entire First Army in France; and in this capacity became renowned for his work on poison gas.

But William Hume's sojourn in France was ultimately memorable for a quite different reason. It was here that he met his future wife, Marie Elisabeth Tisseyre, always known as Mimi.

> Hume and I (wrote Dr Bedson in *The Lancet* of 9th January 1960) were billeted together in Wimereux, next door to . . . a refugee French family from Lille. Friendship with our French neighbours prospered, and much of our leisure time was spent enjoying the delightful hospitality of Madame Tisseyre and her family.

Mimi Tisseyre was a pretty, vivacious girl of seventeen. She, her mother and sister, Germaine, had fled to Wimereux in the Pas de Calais to escape the advancing German armies. Her father, a colonel in the French Army, was fighting in the front line, having left his family in the house of his parents-in-law who owned a linen factory in Lille. It was from this house, shortly to be occupied by the Germans, that Madame Tisseyre and her daughters had fled.

When Mimi began taking English lessons with William Hume's landlady in Wimereux, she and the tall, blue-eyed, thirty-five-year-old Northumbrian fell in love. Neither family was delighted. Apart from the seventeen-year age gap, there were the differences in nationality, language and religion to contend with. When Mimi and her family went off to Tunisia to rejoin her father (twice-wounded in action), everybody must have hoped that the relationship would soon be forgotten.

But Mimi's mind was made up; both she and William were determined to marry. Bowing to the inevitable, Madame Tisseyre accompanied her daughter to Newcastle in August 1918, to cast an eye over the place and to meet her future in-laws. As they emerged from Newcastle station into the grime and poverty of the streets, under a damp, slate-grey sky, Madame Tisseyre was overcome with emotion. 'Mon pauvre enfant', she sighed. 'My poor, poor child. To think that you are to be buried in this awful place.'

Three months later, in November 1918, Mimi and William were married in the Franco-Spanish border town of Hendaye, choosing that area because her father had been sent as a military attaché to Madrid, and had a house in St Jean de Luz. The bride wore white and all the traditional trimmings, but the ceremony was a simple, informal affair in the sacristy of the church; one of the two witnesses had to be brought in from the street. For their honeymoon, the couple went to Biarritz, notorious in those days as a nest of spies. Only later did William discover that it was, for that very reason, out of bounds to the British Army!

For a few months, pending William's demob, Mimi returned to the family home in Lys-Lannoy, outside Lille. (Both grandparents had died while under house-arrest during the German occupation.) Then early in 1919 Mimi said goodbye to the place she had always thought of as home, and set off for her new life as a doctor's wife in Newcastle, that vast unknown city of north-east England. It was an act of faith in the future.

William was instantly re-absorbed into the rigorous life of a consulting physician, who was at the same time a lecturer in pharmacology and medicine, and a researcher into what was always his main interest, cardiology. He and Mimi moved into his father's old house, 4 Ellison Place, whose windows actually overlooked the medical school. It was an elegant, four-storey, terraced house in a Georgian square, in that part of town which was Newcastle's equivalent of London's Wimpole or Harley Streets. In those days it was vital for doctors to live in the town centre, as near as possible to tram or train stops, for the Newcastle catchment area was wide, and many of the patients had long distances to travel.

The French cook whom Mimi brought with her did not long endure the miseries of an unheated house, nor the spartan British existence, with its seemingly incessant demands for consoling cups of tea. She soon returned home to France and to central heating, leaving poor Mimi with nobody to speak French to – until, that is to say, the children came on the scene.

Madeleine, Christine, George and Frances were all born within the space of five years. John came four years later, in 1928, and was always regarded as 'the baby' by the others. All five had names which could be pronounced just as easily in French as in English, and all of them grew up speaking French as naturally as English. Mimi always spoke

French to them (a matter of some embarrassment when they were travelling on the Newcastle trams), switching to English only when William was around. William had never found time in his busy life to master the intricacies of French.

George, who had inherited his father's piercing blue eyes, is generally agreed to have been an exceptionally good baby, who almost never cried. 'He was an attractive child, always more outgoing than the rest of us,' says Christine. 'Right from babyhood, he always loved to make people smile.' When he was born, an under-nurse came to join the staff at 4 Ellison Place, which until then had consisted of a cook (plain British), a housemaid, a parlourmaid, and 'Nurse', together with William's secretary, Mr Dillingham (very much a part of the family), Blair, the chauffeur who came in each day, and Mrs Storey, who came twice a week to do the household laundry. Mimi was an excellent organizer and a strict disciplinarian. Since she insisted on her house being spotless, the housemaid was required to dust the stairs twice every day.

The whole household revolved around William and his professional needs. His consulting rooms were on the spacious ground floor, and the family lived 'above the shop'. The children slept in the attics – 'it was freezing cold up there' – or, when they were very young, with Nurse on the floor below. As the nursery was on the third floor, immediately above the drawing room, they were under strict orders not to make much noise. Once they so far forgot themselves as to make the chandelier in the drawing room shake. For this they were in deep disgrace, but nothing like as deep as on the day they batted a cricket ball straight through the window of the consulting room, where their father was treating a patient for heart trouble! (They were not as a rule allowed to play outside in the small back courtyard which had once been a stableyard; but on that particular day the heat was so stifling that an exception had been made.)

Yet in spite of the discipline (not at all excessive by the standards of the time), the children enjoyed an extraordinarily happy home life. The house itself offered excitement, with its capacious cellars and attics. The window on the back staircase overlooked the medical school, and they loved to watch the students, especially during Rag Week. Three doors away was the Lord Mayor's Mansion House (terraced just like their own), and the children would press their noses to the nursery window when the great parades went by: the annual Empire Day parade, with Boy Scouts, the Boys' Brigade, St John's Ambulance and others, all in uniform. Even more exciting was the time of the Assizes, when the visiting Judges, resplendent in their robes and wigs, rode out from the Mansion House in their open carriages, preceded by a fanfare of trumpets.

For lessons, the whole family went next door to the Drummonds' house, where there was more room. Ann Drummond was roughly the same age as the older Hume girls, and since her 'Nanny' was less strict than the Humes' 'Nurse', and since, being an only child, Ann had more toys than they did, visits to the top-floor nursery at the Drummonds' were regarded as fun. Even lessons had a certain spice, no thanks, however, to the Hume governess, Miss Conway, who was entrusted with the children's education. This lady – 'extremely old-fashioned and a bit alarming' – relied on books that had long been out of date, *Little Arthur's History of England* and the Victorian *Reading Without Tears*. The children did copy-book writing, learned their multiplication tables, and committed poems to memory. When they were naughty, Miss Conway sent them to stand in a corner, a punishment they rather enjoyed, since the corner was next to a window that overlooked the street below.

Twice a day they were taken by Nurse for walks, usually to the parks, where they ran around or played with hoops. Sometimes, on wet days, they were allowed down to Fenwick's in the main shopping street, to the Grainger Market or even (more rarely) to the Laing Art Gallery. Even more occasionally, they walked as far as the town moor, where each year in June, during Newcastle Race Week, that an enormous fair was held, the biggest fair in Europe, it was said. As a special treat, the Hume children were given money and allowed to attend.

Madeleine and Christine liked to save up their pocket money for the occasional riding lesson on the moor, but George went with them only under duress. 'I remember him once being on a large chestnut', laughs Christine. 'The girths weren't properly fastened, and he slithered off, clinging on upside down, just like a circus monkey.'

Indifferent to horse-riding though he may have been, George was nevertheless a keen sportsman. Football was a passion he shared with his father, and both of them were ardent Newcastle United supporters. (Years later when, as Cardinal, George was given the Freedom of the City, along with former Newcastle captain, Jackie Milburn, he asked the footballer for his autograph with all the eagerness of a teenage fan.)

Every Sunday, when the children were small, William Hume played golf. But later, as arthritis took hold, he gave up golf for fishing, an enthusiasm he passed on to his elder son. William had a rod on the Tweed for salmon-fishing, and there was a little loch where he and George went fly-fishing for trout. Conscious that George was a boy surrounded by sisters (John was still a baby), William attempted to introduce a more masculine influence into the boy's life by arranging for a carpenter to come and teach him woodwork. The experiment was a lamentable failure. 'George', say his sisters, 'was always hopeless with his hands.'

He was a happy, home-loving child, the 'clown' of the family, always able to entertain the others and make them laugh. As a self-contained group of children with few ready-made toys, the young Humes were thrown back on their own considerable imaginative resources, amusing themselves by dressing up, putting on plays and variety shows, performing charades. The Christmas pantomime, organized very proficiently by Madeleine (and with an official programme typed by Mr Dillingham), was the high spot of their year, watched by a captive audience of Mimi, Mrs Drummond, Nurse and the under-nurse. On these occasions, George and Christine were the extroverts, clowning and hamming their way through the performance with panache; while John made his contribution by turning somersaults over a broom-handle. They all had stage names, but only John's – Valentine Septic – is still remembered (or confessed to).

Every Christmas they were taken to see the professional panto at the Theatre Royal or the Empire Theatre. Once they also went to Peter Pan, and on another memorable occasion were allowed to go to a music-hall staged in the local 'flea-pit'. The theatre, alas, lived down to its evil reputation, and as the children all 'caught something', they were banned from going there ever again.

On Christmas mornings, the Humes all went to the Infirmary to help their father pass round turkey and Christmas pudding to the patients. Madeleine, older than the rest, noticed that though the women all wore ribbons in their hair and tried to look festive, 'you could see they were fretting about how the family was coping at home without them.'

In fact, all the Hume children had this deep, inbuilt awareness that not everyone was as lucky as they were. These were the hungry Twenties and Thirties, the terrible Depression years, when unemployment was rife in Newcastle and brought poverty and hunger in its wake. The

Infirmary gave eggs away free to needy families; and the police had a 'Boot Fund' to provide shoes and socks for barefoot children.

There were all too many children who went barefoot throughout the bitter winter. Many of them could be seen on a Sunday at Mass in the big Dominican church which the Humes occasionally attended, as a change from their own church, St Andrew's. George, in particular, loved St Dominic's, with its splendid liturgy, its excellent choir and first-class sermons. But St Dominic's stood on the edge of the Newcastle slums, and its large congregation consisted mainly of the deprived: the barefoot children and their mothers, black-shawled, their heads covered with their husbands' cloth caps.

One of the priests from St Dominic's, Father Alfred Pike, was an occasional visitor to Ellison Place – though not too frequent a visitor since, out of deference to William, Mimi did not make a habit of inviting clergy to the house. The Dominican befriended George, and took him along on his visits to the slums, in order to show the boy the terrible conditions in which the poor had to live. One day, they visited a family of twelve who lived all together in a single room, with no food except for 'a tin of ready-mixed tea and sugar sheltering one egg'. George has no doubt that this was a seminal experience for his life: 'I was forced to compare my own good fortune with theirs', he would say later. 'I believe that it was that childhood experience which determined me to become a priest one day.'

His sisters can barely remember a time when George did not want to be a priest. 'Ma', they recall, 'bought him candles, so that he could play at saying Mass.' They love to tell the story of the elderly lady who used to come in to read stories to them, and who would insist that George must marry her when he grew up. One day, he took her on one side and said seriously: 'Jossie, I'm afraid I shan't be able to marry you, because I'm going to be a priest. But if you like, I'll bring you communion on your death-bed instead.'

'He was a wonderful mixture of seriousness and sparkle', remembers his cousin, Phyllis Gibson (formerly Hume). 'When I was eighteen, my mother died and Aunt Mimi invited me to spend Christmas with them. George was only ten at the time, but he showed an amazing gift for sympathy even then. He seemed to know intuitively that I must be missing my mother, and every time he saw me alone, he would come and sit next to me and talk me out of my sadness. I shall always be grateful to him for that – and for his mischievous grin.'

Religion in the Hume household was not intrusive. Mimi respected William's Protestant scruples, and refused to fill the house with the pious paraphernalia favoured by many Catholics. There were no holy pictures, statues or holy water stoups about the place, and no grace was said at meals. William – later Sir William – Hume was not a church-goer, but nor was he an agnostic, as some newspapers asserted at the time of his son's election as Archbishop of Westminster. His wife said that he knelt to say his prayers every night. Later in life, when he was crippled by arthritis, he became friendly with the Vicar of the Jesmond (Newcastle) church, the Rev. Henry Bates, who brought him Holy Communion from time to time.

Mimi herself was a devout Catholic, much more devout, she admitted, than she might have been had she stayed in her native France. When her grandfather, General Tisseyre, died in 1937 (at the age of 98), his hopes for the family were circulated on a memorial card:

> I hope (he had written) that my children and grandchildren will try, as I have done . . . to be good Catholic Christians; and that they will teach their children to be the same. They should tell them that as long as one follows the will of God, no misfortune is beyond repair.

The General must have been proud of his granddaughter, and of the way she taught her children. Yet George, very much influenced by his mother, would later feel that she had taught him to regard God as some kind of super-policeman. He remembered her very first words on the subject. 'Georges,' she had said, 'if you went into a room which was full of apples, and you took one because you were very hungry, GOD WOULD SEE YOU!' It took him a long time to rid himself of the idea of God who watched him and waited to trip him up!

After Miss Conway's death in 1929, the older girls had been sent to school locally, while George and Frances continued in the schoolroom with a governess. Every Saturday morning, they all went for religious instruction at the Marie Reparatrice convent, where each in turn made their First Communion (and where George, years later, would say his first Mass). Frances and George were good friends but, like most children who are constantly thrown together, they fought and teased each other mercilessly. Both children were sent to dancing class. George, despite his great height and gangling walk, was a keen dancer; Frances a most reluctant one. To encourage her daughter, Mimi one day offered a prize for the best dancer – a meringue for tea. George won – but Frances had the last laugh. She got into the nursery before tea-time, and licked all the cream off the outside of the meringue!

Every summer Mimi took the children to her parents' home at Wimereux, where they were joined by her sister, Germaine de Villamil, and her three children. Philippe de Villamil was only six weeks younger than George, and the two were firm friends. (Philippe was drowned in a boating accident in Paris on VE Day.) With their French cousins, the young Humes had a riotous time, 'competing madly on the sands to see who could jump the furthest.' But as time went by and George's legs grew longer, he easily out-jumped them all, and 'the rest of us stopped bothering'.

Sometimes they were sent 'for country life and fresh air' to Wooler, a market town near Alnwick; or to stay with their father's unmarried younger sister, Aunt Betty, in Alston, Cumberland. Aunt Betty was a dog-lover, and the young Humes, who had no pets of their own, were surrounded by them at Alston. Aunt Betty's friends would invite them to tea. One of these, a spinster lady like their aunt, sent them outside first to feed the hens and her pet donkey. 'Well,' said a ravenous four-year-old George, 'we've fed the chickens and the bear (sic!). When are *we* going to eat?'

In the Lake District where at Easter-time they stayed in a large farmhouse and spent all their time out of doors, in all weathers, the children were hungry all the time, especially as the food in the farmhouse was not all it might have been. After a stiff climb one day, George and Ann Drummond, arriving at the snow-line before the others, left a mock farewell note written in the snow on the cliff edge. 'LUNCH WAS THE LAST STRAW!', it said. But a housemaid who accompanied the children on one such holiday, when everything went wrong and 'there was no toilet, no water, no one to cook', reported that George didn't mind at all, just so long as there were plenty of bananas for him to eat!

When George was seven, he went first to the kindergarten of the school attended by his sisters, and then to the Newcastle Prep School, where his father had once been a pupil. Just as in William's day, the boys wore white shirts with Eton collars, and were called 'ring-worms', on account of their black caps ringed with yellow. The Eton collars were too much for the local council school youngsters, who would lie in wait for the 'ring-worms' and attack them. After one such experience, George, though the school was only a short walk from his home, had thereafter to walk to the nearest tram stop and pay the half-penny fare to school.

On the whole, as a Catholic excluded from the Scripture lessons, George Hume felt rather out of things at the Newcastle Prep School, though the Head, Rutland Cumberlege, was a great friend of his father's, and Mrs Cumberlege was very fond of him. She worried over his sticking-out ears. If he kept them tucked under his cap, she urged him, they might grow closer to his head.

His two years at the Prep School did see one small but significant triumph. George played rugby football for the first time, and made quite an impression. 'I never recall my father being so proud and delighted', says Madeleine, 'as when Mr Cumberlege rang to tell him that George had the makings of a first-class rugby player!'

In September 1933, the ten-year-old George went away to school, to Gilling Castle, the prep school for Ampleforth College, a leading Roman Catholic public school run by the Benedictine order of monks. At Gilling, just across the valley from the College, George was completely happy. No longer did he have that sense of isolation which had afflicted him as a Catholic at the Newcastle Prep School: here at last he belonged. (He had not, however, escaped the tyranny of the Eton collar, since at Gilling, and later at Junior House, it was part of the uniform, at least on Sundays.)

Ampleforth, with its bracing air and the opportunities offered by its two thousand acres of open space, suited George perfectly. It is hard to imagine any boy being unhappy in such an idyllic place. The College nestles in the Vale of Mowbray, not far from York, on the southern slopes of the Hambleton Hills and close to the beautiful North Yorkshire moors. A relatively small school, known affectionately to its five hundred or so pupils as 'The Shack', the College provided a family atmosphere and plenty of freedom for its boys. And, though it encouraged sport and a healthy outdoor life, it was not depressingly 'hearty'. Life there, however, was spartan, and there were few luxuries. 'You were damned lucky if you got a hot bath once a week', remembers an old boy – though he admitted that there were showers after Games. 'A pretty austere place', the late Patrick O'Donovan once described it in the Thames Television film 'Basil Hume OSB':

> very inadequately heated . . . Comfortable it was not, and there was a good deal of hardship in the way we went in for appalling runs through the snow, and rugby in the snow. There weren't any concessions to feeble humanity. It wasn't cruelty, just profoundly English. Energetic, healthy, no dilly-dallying about, not too much intellectualism, not too much florid piety.

At the time George Hume became a pupil there, Ampleforth had a remarkable headmaster, Father Paul Nevill, a man of outstanding vision, who was in the process of transforming this small north country school into an educational establishment of national significance. 'Posh Paul', the boys called him – a bit of a snob, no doubt, but immensely approachable and understanding.

After two years in Gilling, George crossed the valley to Junior House, the equivalent of the top forms of any prep school. To Junior House came many boys from other schools, and here George would meet those who would be his companions for the next six years. The headmaster, Father Illtyd Williams, was, according to Father Martin (then Tony) Haigh, 'a marvellous man, full of common-sense', who provided his boys with a well-balanced foundation for life, and created a happy atmosphere in the House. As indeed did the other monks, Fathers Peter and Pascal, and Hugh Dinwiddy, a layman who lived in Junior House. Father Illtyd kept open house and the boys would congregate in his study during their recreation time, playing cards or games or just generally getting to know each other – and Father Illtyd. Even at such an early age, they learned to treat the monks as friends.

Hugh Dinwiddy, who had recently graduated from Cambridge, taught the boys, amongst other things, School Certificate History. George Hume, he remembers, was quiet and sensitive, 'self-confident without being pushy', a popular boy who made friends easily, yet who was not notably a joiner. 'I somehow always knew that George would be a priest', says Dinwiddy. 'In spite of his popularity, he was a boy apart. He seemed not to take part in the usual clubs and social groups. Yet there is a paradox here. At the same time he was captain of Junior House rugby, and was always right in the middle of a scrum.' Dinwiddy, who taught the boys the history of the Reformation, remembers that George was troubled to learn of the hatred and intolerance of that unhappy period. Perhaps because of his own Protestant father, he hated to think of the Christian Church suffering such a deep and painful division. On reflection, Dinwiddy thinks that George's later concern for ecumenism could have stemmed from his study of this period of history, and the conversations that arose from it.

When the time came for George to enter the College proper, he was assigned to a new House, Dunstan's. Ampleforth had six Houses, each of them called after a north country saint, and each caring for fifty or sixty boys. Dunstan's was in the charge of Father Oswald Vanheems, a disciplinarian, but a man of great integrity who won the admiration of his boys, themselves a very distinguished group, hand-picked for the new House. The House was the hub of each boy's life: here were his friends, here his social life and point of reference. If he didn't get on with his housemaster, there were always other monks around for consultation or consolation.

After three years with the Benedictines, George was by now completely at home with them, and readily took to the religious practice of the College. Morning Mass at 7.15 was compulsory.

> You went to Mass every morning (says John Ryan, famous as the creator of Captain Pugwash) unless you had a jolly good reason for not going. And when you got down to the crypt, there were all the monks saying their private Masses at different altars. There was that unforgettable noise that someone called 'the sacred mutter of the Mass'. On Sundays there was evening Benediction as well. And Vespers. Gregorian chant echoed in our ears. We were saturated with the liturgy.

'The Abbey church', echoes Hugh Dinwiddy, 'was the centre of the whole community. The presence of the monks was part of the very air you breathed.'

Those who remember George at that time recall him as 'a nice chap', 'a good all-rounder', but 'nothing remarkable'. He was 'no fool' at lessons, but not brilliant either. His reports were adequate rather than glowing, and bespoke a conscientious plodder. Father Martin Haigh springs to his friend's defence. 'Not a first-class mind, perhaps,' he says, 'but at least a very good second-class one.' George himself reckoned he usually came eighth, ninth or tenth in the class lists – 'at the lower end of the best lot'.

In sport it was a different story. Because of slight astigmatism, he did not play cricket, but he excelled at running and hurdling, and was a high scorer at rugby. At sixteen (1939) he was already in the College's First XV, the youngest in the side by far. The following year, he was made captain. 'He was fast and handled the ball well,' says Father Martin Haigh, 'but he wasn't really a great rugby player. But he *was* a great leader. Everyone in the team would have died for him.' Cecil Foll, a member of the team who became one of George's greatest friends, remembers that it was 'a fantastically happy side, most of whose members have kept in touch with each other and with our captain ever since.'

George was indeed a natural leader, a good judge of

people and an excellent mixer. Though still a non-joiner, his popularity was high, and for some unexplained reason he seems to have been the only boy in the school who was known by his Christian name and not his surname. 'There was something about him', reflects Hugh Dinwiddy, who was then the rugby coach:

> It was a sort of natural 'centred-ness'. All his friends were creative and clever, but most of them were uncertain about what they wanted to do with their lives. George was the only one who *knew*. His decision had already been made.

His friends teased him that one day he would be Headmaster of Ampleforth, or even Abbot. But under the teasing there was a half-sense that such things were truly possible. It is said that the Headmaster, Father Paul, while showing George's mother round the Abbey church one day, pointed to the Abbot's stall and said: 'One day your son will sit there.'

Yet despite such high seriousness, George had not lost his love of fun. On the surface at least he was a happy extrovert, who loved playing the fool and was a clever mimic. He took part in one or two school plays, playing very minor roles – a Russian officer in *Arms and the Man*, a police constable in *I Killed the Count*. But music-hall slapstick, reminiscent of those childhood pantomimes enacted by the family in Newcastle, was more in his line; and he is better remembered for his part in the variety show produced by John Ryan in November 1939, in aid of wartime charities. 'We were all on edge, waiting to go off to the war', says Ryan. 'The variety show was one way of helping.'

The boys gave ten performances in six months, in different parts of the country. George sang a duet, 'Whiskers', with John Ryan, in which he was the stooge who constantly interrupted the latter's attempts to sing a ballad. 'It wasn't that he was wildly funny, but somehow he was the sort of person you recruited for that kind of thing', says Ryan.

Years later, Cardinal Hume recalled the experience on TV in the film, 'Basil Hume OSB':

> I did a sort of farcical number with another chap . . . We were a couple of schoolgirls and we sang a Gilbert and Sullivan song with specially written words:
>
> I'm called little Annabelle,
> Dear little Annabelle,
> though I never can tell why.
> The size of my figger
> gets bigger and bigger . . .
>
> I can't remember the next line.

Cecil Foll, who was Lizabelle to George's Annabelle, and who was short and plump where George was long and skinny, gives his friend credit for a better memory than that would suggest:

> When about three years ago I lunched *à deux* with the Cardinal at Westminster, we sang a verse or two and he was word perfect. As we entered the last chorus, the door behind him opened a fraction, and the horrified face of a nun appeared – and rapidly disappeared again.

Foll also remembers the time when they gave the show in a lunatic asylum, and 'George persuaded the audience to join in a sing-song, and then we couldn't get them to stop.' The *Ampleforth Journal* of September 1940 recorded an even more untoward effect at an army camp, when

> Cecil Foll and George Hume, our glamorous, giggling schoolgirls, paid the penalty for going down into the audience, for they were kissed by two soldiers!

The last two years of George's schooldays were hung over

by the shadow of the war. Increasingly, the pages of the *Ampleforth Journal* were filled with lists of serving officers from the school, and with lengthening lists of casualties. School activities had more and more reference to the war. George became an active member of the Debating Society, an institution which was very important in Ampleforth life, and which had an exclusive claim to Sunday evenings. Among the subjects proposed in 1941 were:

> THAT the sending of an expeditionary force to the continent is necessary for the successful conclusion of the war. (Carried by a large majority.)
>
> THAT woman's place is in the home. (Carried by a small majority.)
>
> THAT this House would prefer Russia as an enemy rather than an ally. (Carried 24–6.)

George Hume was described in the *Ampleforth Journal* as 'a confident and able speaker who, by his clear delivery and persuasive arguments, repeatedly succeeded in winning the support of the House.' Once, when a speaker had aroused the House's wrath, someone shouted impatiently: 'Is Mr X going to resign? If not, why not?' George rose to his feet and, amid general mirth, countered: 'No, Mr X is not going to resign. So what?'

The war impinged in practical ways. Ampleforth had its own version of Dad's Army. As Cecil Foll relates:

> During late 1940 or early 1941, it was the custom for two of the monitors and a member of the Community to spend certain nights 'protecting' Ampleforth from attack by German parachutists. Together with Father Terence, who was in charge of rugby football, George Hume and I made up one such gallant team, whose task was to defend Oswaldkirk Hill. George and I were armed with ancient Lee-Enfield rifles (plus three bullets each – the Germans were not expected in strength!) ; and

> our Reverend sergeant had an enormously long and inefficient torch. The defence technique was for George and myself to station ourselves at the top of the hill – lying each side of the road in a ditch – while Father Terence lurked in the bushes at the bottom of the hill. When a vehicle appeared, Father Terence was expected to sprint behind it as it slowed down to make its ascent, and make a note of the registration number. Since the light of the torch worked only intermittently and his fitness left a lot to be desired, Father Terence seldom arrived at the top with the required information. Even if he had the number, he was usually speechless and near to apoplexy after his exertions.
>
> Needless to say, his guardians, posted to provide covering fire for him, were by this time writhing on the ground in convulsions of mirth. Many a local must have been scared out of his wits when he looked in his rear mirror and saw this enormous red-faced fiend in hot pursuit of him, waving a flashing light.

George was already looking beyond the war, wondering about the kind of world that lay ahead. He aired his own ideas in the Senior Historical Society, of which in 1941 he was the President. 'On the topic of post-war reconstruction', reported the *Ampleforth Journal*:

> G. H. Hume proposed forming a militant Catholic laity whose duty it would be to spread the Faith and uphold the social structure of the country, and so prevent a general state of chaos spreading over the world at the end of the war.

He felt strongly on this subject. As a school Monitor, whose main function it was to set a good example to the younger boys, George took his responsibilities as a Christian very sincerely indeed. His concern for the sort of world that lay beyond the peace caused him to worry about the poor quality of religious teaching in the school, about the boring, lack-lustre way in which Religious Instruction was put over. RI lessons frequently broke up in general mayhem and disorder. To counteract the inevitable decline of interest in religion, George, with a group of young rugby players and their friends, using Hugh Dinwiddy as a point of reference, formed themselves into a group calling itself 'The Movement', in which each member tried to live his own faith more fully and to deepen his Christian commitment; and also tried to persuade others to follow his example. At the same time the group attempted to bring pressure to bear on the monks, to persuade them to improve their teaching techniques and make religion come alive.

Unlike the Jesuits, the Benedictines did not like sodalities and 'élitist' societies. So George found himself summoned to Father Paul's study to explain himself. This he did so effectively that he emerged from the interview with Father Paul's full permission to continue with what he was doing. Never before, said the Headmaster later, had he encountered a boy of such discernment or such clear-headed understanding of what he was about.

As the time drew near for him to leave his schooldays behind, George had every need of such clear-headedness and discernment. For he now faced an agonizing decision about his immediate future. The problem was twofold. The war was going badly and there was a real pessimism about its outcome. It seemed possible that the Germans would actually invade Britain. Given this situation, should he follow his vocation to be a priest – or join the army and risk losing that vocation? And if he chose to follow his vocation, what kind of vocation was it? As a child he had imagined that it was to the energetic, passionately intellectual Dominicans; but his years with the less flamboyant and less individualistic Benedictines had left their mark. He decided to consult his Games Master, Father Anthony Ainscough, about the first problem.

> He came down to see me because he was very worried (recalls Father Anthony). He felt a loyalty and sense of duty to the services, yet felt he was called to be a monk. What should he do? I said to him: 'There's no yardstick for judging a problem of this sort. Whichever decision you make will be the right one. We need the army, but we need spiritual people too.'

Father Anthony suggested that he talk with a layman, and George, as so often before, turned to Hugh Dinwiddy. To Dinwiddy he presented the problem in its full scope, confessing his inability to decide between the rival claims of Dominicans and Benedictines. Hugh Dinwiddy sensed that George was temperamentally more suited to the Benedictine life, but was inclined to think that he needed the sharper intellectual stimulus which the Dominicans could provide. The decision could only be for George to make. George returned to Father Anthony, who dismissed Dinwiddy's objections. 'If you decide to come here, and prove to have the potential,' he said, 'you'll get the right training, never fear. Now, go away and think about it some more.'

George did as he was asked, and eventually opted for the Benedictines, deciding, moreover, to enter the monastery immediately. Reflecting on that decision many years later (Thames TV film), the Cardinal told broadcaster Robert Fleming:

> I had a kind of boyish idea that we were going to be invaded, and that priests and people like me would all be strung up on lamp-posts. It seemed like a different kind of heroism.

Then he added: 'But if I had the decision to make again, I would have gone to the war.' Father Martin Haigh, who took the same difficult decision at the same time, does not agree. He describes that decision as 'a tremendous act of faith. We were affirming that we would serve our country better in the monastery than on the battlefield.'

But George's closest friends did not see it that way. They had not even considered the possibility that George would not go into the army for the duration of the war. For them the issue was clear cut. When his friend, John Johnston, told George that he had been accepted into the Grenadier Guards, he asked him which regiment he (George) had applied for. 'To my surprise he told me he was going into the monastery, and I could not resist chiding him for doing such a thing in wartime.' Cecil Foll writes of his 'tremendous shock' at finding that George was to enter the novitiate instead of joining up. He himself was to join the navy, and tried hard to persuade George to change his mind.

But the time of George's indecision was over, and he could not be deflected. With Father Paul's advice – 'never lose your sense of humour' – ringing in his ears, George Hume entered the Benedictine noviciate and received the name by which he would henceforth be known – Basil.

2

The Monastic Years

The Benedictine Way

This chapter is concerned not merely with the Cardinal's private life but inevitably with the private life of his 'family', the Community of Ampleforth; 'his private life' in the sense of their inner life of the spirit, the growth of that life. It was there that the inward journey began in earnest. The Abbot holds not only the 'secrets of the King' which are his own, but also the 'secrets' of the brethren, their spiritual struggles, defeats and victories. This can only be an interim report, as it were, from the outside, for we have to wait – whoever is granted the time – until his death for 'The Life' proper. This can be but sketches, snap-shots, meagre fare.

The Benedictines have been part of English life from the time of the Anglo-Saxons, whom they converted. Around the time also of Edward the Confessor, buried in the old Benedictine Abbey church of Westminster, most of the early bishops of England were Benedictines. It should, therefore, not seem odd that Pope Paul VI should choose another English Benedictine to be Archbishop of the Catholic Archdiocese of Westminster. And yet . . .? A monk, an archbishop, and in the modern world?

It could be argued that the upsurge of spontaneous enthusiasm which greeted the appointment in February 1976, which encouraged the BBC both to televise the ceremony and ordination service and to repeat the transmission three days later, was in part due to a subconscious awareness of the importance of monastic tradition in the life of the English people. The seal was put on this by the wonderful silence and prayerful serenity of Westminster Abbey as monks and people welcomed him into the Abbey on the very day of his consecration.

Abbot Basil, in his last sermon to the boys at Ampleforth on 22nd February 1976 said:

> I am only moving to Westminster because I have been an Abbot of Ampleforth. A trick of history sees me as head of this Community . . . what I am is what you have given. And I have been responsible for a very wonderful Community, but a human one.

Some of those who chance to read this book may know little of monks or monasteries; yet they probably know that Cardinal Basil Hume considers himself to be a monk still, and may often be seen dressed as one. For thirty-five years the Benedictine monastery of Ampleforth in Yorkshire was his home, and the Community there was his family. It was from his position as Abbot – leader and father of that Community – that he was chosen to be Archbishop of Westminster. It is the Benedictine life which has formed his spirituality and to some extent his character: 'You remain a monk', Pope Paul VI reminded him when he became a Cardinal. So, to begin to understand him, one needs to grasp something of what it has meant for him to be a monk, to be a Benedictine, to be an Abbot.

A wise old monk at Ampleforth, Father Placid Dolan, once said that the history of a monastery could be written on a postage stamp. What a microscopic stamp must be required for the history of an individual monk, even Father Basil Hume! But he has broken out of the enclosed world of the monastery to become an actor on a world stage. His origins, therefore, become interesting, even intriguing.

While we easily imagine the early life of a Harold Wilson or of a Mrs Thatcher, here, so people say, is someone who went off and buried himself in a monastery until the age of fifty-three. Only then was he dragged out into the public eye and into the rarified air of Westminster as Archbishop.

Though the style of the Benedictine life varies considerably from one age or from one community to another, the essential characteristic of a monastery is to be a place of prayer, study and work. There all is directed to one end: the search for God. The means to this end will vary, but among the means are the three vows, quite distinct from those taken by members of more recent Orders. They are Stability, Conversion of Manners and Obedience.

Stability in practice means, throwing in one's lot for life – as in marriage – with this particular monastic family.

Conversion of Manners (*Conversio*, or *conversatio morum*) has the meaning of acceptance of the monastic way of life according to the way expressed in the Rule of St Benedict and the sound customs of the particular monastery.

Obedience, whose meaning is clear enough, is more all-embracing than it seems at first sight: obedience to God as expressed by the Rule and the Abbot and the members of the Community. The more standard vows today are Poverty, Chastity and Obedience. The first two are implicit in the vow *conversio morum*.

Brother Basil must have learned early how to be a community-man. The word 'monk' comes from a Greek word meaning 'alone', and in early Christian parlance, unmarried, celibate. That did not mean emotionless. There are many places in *Searching for God* when Father Basil expresses surely his own experience of how to reach the balance between loving too much and not loving at all, neither allowing affections to dominate nor, from fear, crushing them altogether.

The general pattern of Benedictine monastic life has

remained the same, whether we look at St Benedict's own monastery at Monte Cassino in the sixth century, at St Dunstan's at Canterbury in 1000 or Durham in 1500 at the two ends of the Middle Ages, or at a monastery today. The hours of wakefulness, apart from meals, are divided between prayer, study and work. The exact times of prayer and the quantity have varied; the quantity sometimes much more, as at Cluny or Durham, sometimes less, as in most modern monasteries. But in every case the public prayer is drawn from the Psalter and from passages from both Old and New Testaments. Abbot Basil advised his monks to read those Psalms privately and slowly, for example Psalms 41 and 62, if they were beginning to find their enthusiasm was flagging. Every day monks praise God together in choir, in the early morning at Matins; at about sunrise at Lauds; round about noon at Midday Office; before nightfall at Vespers or Evensong; before bedtime at Compline. The study will vary as the monk progresses; at first of course, the Rule and the Psalms, the history of the Order; then Scripture – *Lectio divina* – Philosophy and Doctrine, these partly secular; then the great spiritual authors – all these, for a monk, a ruminating study in hand with God.

Work will take on numerous forms, from looking after the material affairs of the monastery to spiritual conferences to Trappists, manual work in orchard, garden or field, then teaching. At Ampleforth the monks run a school. Brother Basil put his heart into this last work, not as a disagreeable chore, but as a work of God and for Him, sharing in His creativity, leading boys to find God, and teaching them to teach themselves. But Basil never forgot his private prayer, being with God in faith.

When in 1940 the young George Hume took the monastic habit at Ampleforth as Brother Basil, he joined a monastery whose life, then as now, was based on the Rule of St Benedict: a rule written fifteen hundred years ago, so old and yet so new, like the Gospel of Jesus which is its model. For the young, historically-minded novice-to-be, his choice had the added attraction that Ampleforth claimed an unbroken continuity back to the forty monks who were sent from Rome by St Gregory the Great and reached the Isle of Thanet in 598. For the Ampleforth monks came to England from Dieulouard in Lorraine at the time of the French revolution, where they had been settled as a community of English monks since the reign of James I, linked directly to the ancient pre-Reformation Abbey of Westminster. It was fitting, therefore, that in the evening of the day on which Father Basil was ordained Archbishop of Westminster, monks from Ampleforth and many other Benedictine monasteries were invited by the Dean to sing Vespers in the Abbey, as their spiritual forebears had done for so many hundreds of years before – an invitation repeated in 1980, when the monks of Ampleforth, and from elsewhere, sang the Vespers of St Benedict there to mark the fifteenth centenary of his birth.

Learning to be a Monk

Young George arrived back at Ampleforth after his last school summer holiday in 1941 with little luggage – some old clothes for manual work, a few socks and shirts, a Bible, a Rule of St Benedict and as little else as possible. As the old Novice Master used to say, 'As for poverty, see what you can do without.' At York Station Hotel he and his future companions had their last convivial drink as laymen, then took the local train, passing Alne, Coxwold and Ampleforth to disembark at Gilling. They came to the Abbey via Oswaldkirk, not knowing what to expect.

Their cells – rooms – way up at the top of the building, were furnished each with a bed, table, hard chair, tin basin, wash-hand-stand, large jug for collecting water, tumbler, bar of soap and a gorgeous view from the window. St

Benedict himself did not propose that his monks should sleep on the floor. Simplicity rather than austerity reigned: 'Let each receive bedding suitable to their manner of life' (C 22). 'Let no one presume . . . to have anything as his own – anything whatever, whether book or tablets or pen or whatever it may be – since they are not permitted to have even their bodies or wills at their own disposal . . .' (C 33). However, 'for bedding, let this suffice: a mattress, a blanket, a coverlet and a pillow' (C 33). This did not seem extreme to the young George. Now, at first, there was a touch of almost romantic excitement about it all. But at the same time, there was a cold sense of leaving home.

After a week's retreat given by the novice master, with two or three talks a day, the novices were required to kneel before the Abbot and Community in their lay clothes – bright shirts and ties, smart jackets, coloured socks – and answer the curt question: 'Why have you come?'

George found it difficult to give an answer without writing a book. Finally he said, 'To seek God'.

Those words were still in his head when he chose the title of his first book, *Searching for God*, in 1977. They are echoed in what St Benedict says of the novice master, that he shall be 'A senior monk . . . skilled in winning souls, to watch over them with the utmost care. *Let him examine whether the novice is truly seeking God*' (C 58).

The old Abbot gave a little talk, a mixture of encouragement and warnings. After this George took off his bright tie and smart jacket, to be clothed in the monastic habit – as no doubt St Bede had been and St Wilfrid, St Boniface and St Anselm in centuries past – and became Brother Basil. He and his fellow novices were given new names to signify a new life. St Basil the Great, after whom Brother Basil was named, was the great bishop of Caesarea in Asia Minor (AD 330–80), champion of orthodoxy, and not afraid of learning. He had 'graduated' from the University of Athens, as the young Basil would graduate from Oxford. He had been a monk and founder of monasteries before becoming a bishop. He was a reconciler, a peace maker.

Meanwhile, there was Brother Basil with four or five other like-minded young men, cut off from the outer world in order to rediscover another, the inner world, in which God was, and also where their own real being was: to know God and self, as St Augustine would put it, a unique opportunity for silence, for prayer, and for study in the ancient sense of meditation on the great truths.

When Brother Basil's light was burning at its dimmest in those first years, he went to his novice master and said, 'I can see no light.'

'You have not come to enjoy yourself', was the reply.

'No, but I feel I am being buried.'

'You are!' said the Novice Master. He was not as harsh as this sounds.

The novice master at that time was Father David Ogilvie Forbes, whose influence on Brother Basil was paramount, at least for the first two formative years (1941–43). He had been his confessor before he entered the novitiate. Father David was a younger son of a twice-married Anglican missionary who had been received into the Church in middle life, and retired with considerable wealth to Boyndlie, in Aberdeenshire, where he raised a numerous family. Father David, a Highlander, and very holy in an extremely simple way, was decidedly not scintillating, and his voice had in it the drone of the bagpipes. He must have been a strain on the youthful, lively Brother Basil. But Father David was of the mettle saints are made of. With his single-minded pursuit of holiness went great understanding, gentleness, and simplicity of outlook: obedience, humility, silence, all led to prayer. For all his gloomy voice, these were precisely what the mind needed when it could have gone chasing after glittering non-essentials. He cared very much for his novices. He seemed to be the perfect monk, though he had slipped up on one famous occasion, when in his own noviciate he had swallowed down, on the spur of the hungry moment, a whole dish of cakes meant for a football team tea. (He confessed it to his novice master, but probably not later to his own novices.)

Brother Basil also came into contact with another senior monk, gruff in speech, sensitive of spirit, Father Placid Dolan. In one of those moments of desperation that the young experience, he went to him to say simply, 'I am going.'

'No you are not', came the reply.

'Well, then, I shall go on the Feast of the Immaculate Conception.'

'No, I'm going away, wait here till I come back.'

Father Placid went away. He became exceedingly ill. He never came back. Brother Basil stayed.

There was more to Father Placid than that small incident, however. He had a joyous spirit, imbued with the conviction of faith that grace was God's own life in us, and that we lived in the new world of the Resurrection. Hope was a great active virtue for him. He was of the spirit of the Second Vatican Council, long before it happened.

We need not go very far to know what being a monk meant and means to Basil Hume the monk, it is plain to read in his book, *Searching for God*. The aims he there puts to the novices and to the Community are his own. Repeatedly he stresses the importance of not taking as the end, goal or purpose of monasticism things which are only means: the accumulation of virtues, even regular observance, certainly not a humble mien, even the Liturgy. He maintained that to be a monk is to search for God. Of course, that is what being a Christian is too, a pilgrim looking for God; but a monk does so in a special setting. It is easy to be so concerned about the setting as to forget the very purpose of it all: finding God in life. Not that God can ever be fully discovered – it is a life-long journey.

Father Basil could talk and write about the rough road,

even its occasional grimness, but those were just the negative elements of 'the desert'. He wrote far more about where God lurks on our journey towards him, the glimpses granted through that cloud of unknowing; how God 'appears' in our failures, in our weaknesses, in our community life, in our joys. The noviciate for him was a thrilling experience of discovery. It was also, at times, a frightening discovery of the emptiness of his own self. But he was not dismayed.

It is surprising how mature his understanding of spiritual matters was in those early years of his monastic life. He understood that it consisted in a persistent concentration on union with God in prayer at the centre of our being. For him the picture of the life of a monk is in two parts: the desert where the monk withdraws to search for God, and the market-place where the monk goes to find God's children. At Ampleforth the withdrawal or 'the desert' was the monastery, the individual monastic cell, the choir; the market-place was the classroom, the rugger field, the school Houses, and further afield the Benedictine parishes. St Gregory the Great, the Apostle of England, and St Boniface of Crediton, the Apostle of Germany, both monks, were among his heroes for that reason. He wanted both elements to be presented, the prayerful element and the apostolic one, as parts of the most ancient tradition of the Venerable English Benedictine Congregation.

Brother Basil had been a very active schoolboy, at rugby he was a skilled and tough player, captain of the school team. Once a week in those quiet winter months of the noviciate, he would go off with the other novices to kick a ball about, when no one was around. By his third year he was back helping on the rugger field; he had his first taste of his apostolate as a monk at this early formative time.

At the end of the one-year noviciate he made simple vows; that is, he vowed to make a trial run in the monastery which would last three years. When at the Ampleforth house of studies, St Benet's Hall, Oxford, in 1945, he again had to choose, this time to take the vows to be a monk for life. This he resolutely did, and expected to remain at Ampleforth, or in one of its parishes in Lancashire, Cumberland or South Wales, for the rest of his life. Pope Paul VI, or God acting through him, eventually chose otherwise. For the time being, however, he went on with his studies.

Years of Study

In the first years following his initial noviciate, Brother Basil encountered two monks who influenced his thought considerably. The first was the eccentric and delightful Father Raphael Williams, the brilliant amateur watercolourist, who taught philosophy to the young monks in a very personal manner. From him Brother Basil discovered that he could begin to think in abstractions, and that doing so led somewhere. So when later he found himself studying dogmatic and moral theology at Fribourg, out of the masterpiece of St Thomas Aquinas, the *Summa Theologica*, he felt at home.

The other was Father William Price, later Headmaster of Ampleforth, who had won a first at Oxford in jurisprudence and a second in history in three years. Under him church history became real. A little dull in manner (though touched with irony), Father William's approach was extremely competent and orderly, an excellent training for the young mind. Father William did not succeed in completing the course laid down, which was an outline of church history from the first century to the beginning of the twentieth. He only reached the sixteenth century, a gap Brother Basil found awkward when starting his history studies at Oxford.

Those first years had their lighter side. Life in the noviciate was not all prayer, study and books! There were pleasant interludes of holiday, and one or two incidents of fun survive in the folklore of the place. One was the occasion when Brother Basil and another young monk dressed up as Captain and Mrs Jackson, visiting Ampleforth and hoping to put their boy down for the school. The hoax broke down in laughter when Brother Basil's moustache got unstuck and fell into the teacup. The following morning the Abbot – not in the original plot – greeted him with, 'Good morning, Captain Jackson!' He was one of a band of very lively and cheerful young monks.

Just as in the Middle Ages, the monasteries of England sent some of their monks for further studies to Oxford University, to houses where Worcester and Trinity Colleges now stand, so since the end of last century the English Benedictines have sent their more studious monks to their own small college, St Benet's Hall, Oxford. It was decided that Brother Basil should go there.

St Benet's Hall, 38 and 39 St Giles, a tall, elegant pair of houses from the outside, stands along the west side of the street, at the point where the Banbury and Woodstock Roads slide into each other as they spew traffic through Oxford. Directly opposite the hall is 'The Lamb and Flag', in the distance towards the left, the red brick mass of Keble College, and so to the Parks with their cricket pitches. The rest of the university was way off to the right as you peered out of the upper windows.

In the early part of the nineteenth century some ambitious architect had hoped to build many more 'St Benet's' down the St Giles, but it stands awkwardly, both ends naked, cut off like a cake, the two sides windowless. Numbers 38 and 39 had been a girls' school run by Ursuline nuns, the earliest group of sisters ever to be unenclosed. The interior, in Brother Basil's time, still had the feel of a convent; but the rooms had high ceilings and most were spacious with high, wide windows. The heating, however, in winter, was almost nil. A fire burned in the Common Room. In the garden behind the Hall was a small but devotional chapel; beyond lay Wellington Square.

Over and above the heavy load of reading, lectures, essays and tutorials, the young monks in those days were obliged to participate in a considerable amount of the Divine Office in choir, as well, of course, as the daily Conventual Mass. For some, perhaps amongst them Brother Basil, on a poor wartime diet, the double regime must have been a considerable strain.

It might have seemed obvious that someone who spoke and wrote fluent French, and who had already had some tuition in German, should go up to Oxford to read modern languages. But the senior modern languages master, Father Robert Coverdale (who had an eye on Brother Basil to succeed him), had been transferred from teaching to the Procurator's Office, only to learn after Brother Basil's return from Oxford for the Christmas holidays, that he was already enrolled in the History School.

Father Justin McCann, the Master of the Hall, had for a short time been Prior at Ampleforth. He was a natural scholar and austere in his habits. Father Bede Jarrett, Prior of Blackfriars (also in St Giles) repeatedly advised him to relax his ascetical ways somewhat. He was often unwell; rarely if ever did he take to his bed. His two main interests were Benedictine things and the mystics, notably Father Augustine Baker's *Holy Wisdom* and *The Cloud of Unknowing*, both of which he edited. His life of St Benedict still remains unchallenged. He was also an excellent translator; Karl Adam's *The Spirit of Catholicism* and Abbé Delatte's *Commentary on the Rule of St Benedict*, one from the German, the other from French, he himself considered were his most useful work.

Mr William A. Pantin, an outstanding authority on medieval monasticism and on Oxford's history, Fellow of Oriel College, was one of Brother Basil's tutors. He was an old friend of the Master, Father Justin McCann, with whom he shared a learned interest in the origins of the English Benedictine Congregation; some of their enthusiasm was caught by Brother Basil. 'Billy Pantin' was unique in style. His study was shin-deep in books, and yet the legend is firm that he took his tutorials, not simply standing up but walking back and forth in the room, declaiming, more often than not, his comments and his theories, through the open window – to the empty quad below. His manner was engaging and his matter scholarly. Brother Basil took to him.

It was a widening of horizons for Brother Basil, and he found himself at home in history, as he had done unexpectedly in philosophy. Oxford left this impression upon the young monk: a habit of academic precision and perhaps a slight scholarly scepticism, which fortunately would not be entirely erased by future studies at the Catholic University of Fribourg; also a life-long interest in History.

St Benet's in those days was on the edge of the University, and the young monks, including Brother Basil, felt this, not only physically but psychologically. Rarely did Father Justin allow them out in the evening. But as some relief from work Brother Basil, with others, played a lot of rugby with the Greyhounds and even for the University, although never in an 'away' match. As the University filled up with those coming back from the war and young ones straight from school, competition in sport and study became stronger. The enthusiasts for the game used to gather either at St Benet's, Campion Hall (the Jesuit House of Studies) or Jesus College. Between them they produced a team in 'Cuppers', or inter-college competition, under the umbrella of St Catherine's, an almost entirely clerical and ecumenical side.

For just one day in the three years all monastic restrictions fell away. It was 8th May 1945, VE Day, victory in Europe had been won. The young took to the street, and that evening they commandeered the buses and cabs to celebrate. Somewhere among the delirious mêlée was Brother Basil; and Father Justin searching for his little flock. Brother Basil had one more year to go.

He did well in Finals, considering the limitations of his background studies, receiving second-class honours. But one's impression is that Oxford, for all its historical associations, the beauty of the countryside, and the enjoyment of rugby with the Greyhounds, had its limitations. St Benet's Hall itself, the little Benedictine 'college', was an austere, rather gloomy place at the time. The furnishings might have come from the remains of a sale of a seedy Victorian railway station hotel. As liberty of movement was very restricted there were few opportunities for sharing the ordinary life of the lay undergraduate; and it had been wartime. Brother Basil's lively spirit, if not quenched, was certainly dampened.

So he left the University with deep respect, and with his mind replete with modern political English and European history, perhaps a rather narrow vision of what history is really about. While the French Revolution was his special subject, he also acquired an abiding interest in history in the wider sense, with a special interest in medieval history and in the ancient abbeys of England: Selby, Durham, Rievaulx, Fountains and Westminster. After the heavy work and restrictive atmosphere of Oxford, his mind was now turning to theology, and his spiritual life began to burgeon, nourished, as its studies were mainly to be, on the thought of St Thomas Aquinas.

From Oxford, Brother Basil was sent to study theology at the Catholic University at Fribourg, a picturesque small university town in the Swiss mountains. Its beauty did not on first impact appeal to him, and conditions were so crude and rugged he felt like coming home but did not. He and three other Benedictines were housed in the seminary, the Salesianum. Lectures were in Latin. A bemused Brother

Basil listened excitedly, then dejectedly, as professors spoke the curious mixture of old classical and pragmatic Latin, elucidating Thomas Aquinas, occasionally confusing rather than enlightening. Brother Basil had a succession of Ampleforth contemporaries at Fribourg, but not one of them survived four gruelling years. It says much for Brother Basil's inner strength of will and determination, to say nothing of the developing spiritual insight, that he fought the battle with Latin alone in his cell, working long hours at its translation. It took six months. One morning, in the spring of 1947, he understood a Latin lecture! He has a simple joy in overcoming difficulties. Years later he produced a short classic Latin speech at the Synod of Rome, about a dream. Brother Basil could dream, could be an idealist; but all this has roots in persevering determination and pragmatism – the ground work had to be secure.

Looking back on those years, he found that at Fribourg he really had space to breathe, space to be, space to think, to study. There too, he found St Thomas Aquinas. When asked recently what book he had found, in those early years, the most illuminating for him, the answer was quite simple: St Thomas' *Summa Theologica*. It satisfied his hunger for truth, for order and for loving God. He found his fuel for prayer in the First Part, which is simply on God, '*De Deo Uno*'; and it was the first question of the *Summa*, the Nature of Theology, that is, the study of God Himself, that he chose to write on in the final examination for the licentiate. Archbishop Temple, when he first discovered that great work, found himself laughing with astonishment and pleasure at the amazing intellectual feat, its very structure. Brother Basil, too, was delighted with it. He was also fortunate in his teachers, one of whom was a great Dominican theologian of the day, Father Thomas Deman, who had edited a volume of the famous *Edition des Jeunes* of the *Summa*. He was equally blessed in his Scripture professor, Father F.-M. Braun OP, whose major interest was the study of St John's Gospel – *L'Evangile et les Epîtres de S Jean* (Paris 1953).

For Brother Basil, Fribourg was not only a good place for the study of theology, already open as it was to the new life that would flower at the great Second Vatican Council, and in the full stream of the revival of interest in the work of St Thomas Aquinas; it was also one of the places where the revival of Scripture study was flourishing under the inspiration of the greatest of modern Catholic exegetes, Father Marie-Joseph Lagrange of the Ecole Biblique in Jerusalem, who had died not long before (1938). Perhaps even more important, it was at Fribourg that Brother Basil had the opportunity to share thinking about the Church, about Scripture, and about ecumenism with intelligent young men, like him working towards the priesthood, who came not only from the countries of Europe and America, but also from the young churches of Africa, and those from the Far East. Meanwhile he was becoming familiar with German – Italian was to come later.

From Fribourg too, he was able to visit the Swiss monasteries, especially Einsiedeln, and in Italy, Subiaco. Thus he began to acquire a feel for the spirit of monasteries other than his own and, like other young clerical students from England who lived for a period abroad, studying theology at Louvain, Paris, Strasbourg, Munich and above all Rome itself, he learned to think in European and not just English terms. This breadth of experience and understanding was to be invaluable when in due course he became Abbot of his own Community, and later Archbishop and Chairman of the Council of European Bishops.

But his real introduction to Catholic European thought and even European monasticism, in the widest sense, came much later, when he was already Abbot and was elected Chairman of the International Monastic Ecumenical Commission and that of the similar Commission for Monastic Renewal.

Teacher and Housemaster

In the year 1950 Brother Basil was ordained priest in the Abbey Church. His priesthood as well as his monasticism were and are central to his life. He came back to an Ampleforth, which, after the Second World War, was gathering its forces, its inspiration, to become a school academically able to rival some of the best in the country. But Ampleforth had an added monastic dimension. The school was run by the monks with the help of a strong team of laymen; the monastery itself was in a stage of growth. Father Basil was to have a very considerable part in both sides of that life. He shared the prayer life and enthusiasm of the monks; from 1955 to 1963 he was Professor of Dogmatic Theology to the young monks, and very soon (in 1955) he became a house-master in the school. He was already senior modern languages master, as well as coach of the First XV. His teaching load was formidable: Religion to the Sixth Form, A-Level French prose and literature, as well as A-Level European History.

From his earliest days as a monk, and before, he saw his vocation as one of prayer and apostolic work. He calls it the Mixed Life. Ampleforth has always been dedicated to both prayer and apostolic activity: monastic prayer, prayer in community and activity compatible with that; its long tradition of work on home missions. So for him, teaching or working on our monastic missions was not just sharing in unfortunate necessities, but tremendous God-given opportunities to bring people to God, to Christ. Preaching in particular was for him a veritable vocation. This comes across again and again in his 'conferences', which can be read in *Searching for God*. Thus, as a house-master,

> I was, as the father of this little community, teaching

> its members to live the Christian life and be members of a community. I was there as their priest, as if presiding over a small parish (p. 89).

But he didn't forget the practical details of teaching:

> The art of Schoolmastering can be summed up quite simply: it is to teach boys to teach themselves . . . To teach boys to teach themselves how to live, how to pray, how to work, how to direct their lives . . . (p. 87).

Therefore when he returned to Ampleforth after his studies, he felt he was entering into the work which God had prepared him for.

St Bede's House, 1955–63

As house-master Father Basil saw himself still very intimately linked with the life of the monastery. St Bede's House was then itself not separated from the Abbey under the Abbot. The prayers of the house-master and those of the boys would be consciously linked with the prayers of the monks. The weekly talks would have a basis of monastic virtues – which of course are Christian virtues – turned not directly towards God, but towards the life in the world in which most of the boys were destined to live, for example, the meaning of success, failure, true humility, obedience towards God. It is perhaps not fully appreciated that in a monastic school such as Ampleforth, the house-master's study is also used by the boys, who browse over the dailies and weeklies and the house library books. Father Basil enjoyed house-mastering for that reason, as it gave him close and easy contact with the boys. He saw himself not as a disciplinarian, but rather as a guide, one who gave each boy freedom to act, to think, to grow, yes, even to make mistakes and to learn from them. He was not for pushing religion down their throats, but giving them the opportunity to grow out of childish faith into a strong, virile, yet humble faith in God, and trust in His Church.

At this time the boys saw him as a strenuous energetic man, good at games, good at teaching, hard on himself, spurring the eager, considerate of the timid, with an infectious sense of humour, a drive that carried you along, not aloof but not 'one of the boys' either, yet with that natural command which did not have to be put on. They saw him as a monk, in which there was an element of mystery and restraint. They could see that the Mass and prayer meant more to him than anything else. His being commanded respect, affection and obedience.

Father Basil held a loose rein but was firm when matters of importance were involved, and boys knew where they stood. Pettiness was not the order of the day. Occasionally, once a term or so, there was a sudden hiatus as the housemaster pitched in, brought to the surface troubles and any ill-ordered goings on, dealt with them, and then sat back to observe and monitor – a delicate balance between authority and freedom.

For a short time Father Basil was also curate in Ampleforth village, one of his apostolic works that he found most rewarding. Even after he became Archbishop, on his short visits to Ampleforth he would take himself off and visit his many old friends from those days.

It was then, in about 1960, that he and Father Martin Haigh launched the Ampleforth Pilgrimage to Lourdes, an annual event that still thrives and is a source of grace.

The Abbacy

In April 1963 came a major change in Father Basil's life, when he was elected to succeed Abbot Herbert Byrne as Abbot of Ampleforth. Had this occurred ten years earlier, it would hardly have seemed momentous, even for the monastery itself. But 1963 was no ordinary year – it was the Year of Change. It was the year of the assassination of the President of the United States, John Kennedy. It was the year of the Beatles, and of the upsurge of the young. And it was the year that the first session of the Second Vatican Council ended; the year in which Pope John XXIII died and Paul VI succeeded him. The Church and Pope Paul VI had to live and grapple with the renewal of the life of the Church. Abbot Basil had to grapple with the renewal among his monks, and the renewal of the institution that his abbey was. What should be done?

Had everyone remained calm, no doubt many would have been spared the agonies they experienced, as would Abbot Basil, and so many other abbots and religious communities throughout the Catholic world. But calm was not the order of the day. There were forces let loose which aggravated the tensions and fears, both of those who wanted none of the changes and of those who wanted many. Up to the opening of the Council, the whole Church had been held on a tight rein; almost every event in the Church was governed, controlled from Rome itself. Suddenly a sense of liberation took hold. Many in the Church and in the monasteries and Religious Orders began to behave like adolescents, they wanted to see how far they could go. To be an abbot or prior in those days was no easy honorary post, far from it. It is instructive to consider how Abbot Basil, guided by a shrewd and prudent instinct, sought to steer a course down the rapids while avoiding the rocks on either bank.

But first it is necessary to understand a little more of what a Benedictine monastery is and what kind of an institution Father Basil, as newly elected Abbot, had to deal with. In the first place, the monastic world is a very ancient one. Its roots go back to Roman times, to the age of Rome's decline in the fifth century, an age as troubled and helpless, as threatened by disaster, as our own – for all our wealth and technological power. The spiritual origin of all the Benedictine communities, these compact little societies of which Ampleforth is one, is Benedict of Nursia who was born about 480 and died about AD 547. A self-propelled drop-out, Benedict left the schools of Roman Studies, such as they were, for the rugged foothills of the Appenines, north-east of Rome. He began to live alone in a cave; others joined him; he fled again, this time to Monte Cassino in Southern Italy, half way to Naples. There he established his 'new model' monastery; and there, on the mountain top, he composed his Rule. It contained the wisdom of the man, and was a blue-print for establishing a little society, a monastery, where people could follow Christ to the limit. It started with celibacy. Others could do the same in different ways in the world and in marriage. But like a mountain climber, Benedict and his followers chose to move forward unimpeded by family, or wealth, in order to be ready, like a soldier waiting for orders, a sprinter at the start of a race, to do God's will in any way He chose.

Father Basil was Abbot for thirteen arduous years. One hour as abbot is arduous, since an abbot is not a boss, but the servant, the father of all. Those under him are not children, but men, not saints, but sinners, vowed to the three Benedictine vows, but at times wilful, proud, demanding, in spite of themselves. Therefore his 'fatherhood' is one of compassion, of understanding, of patience, but also of firmness. Each monk he had to love, understand, sympathize with and help in a special way suited to each.

St Benedict is at his best when describing the role of the abbot. Just as this description applied, as St Gregory wrote, to St Benedict himself, so in very large measure did it apply to Abbot Basil. Yet how completely inadequate does any abbot, if he is honest, know himself to be, faced with the picture of the perfect abbot as described in chapters two and sixty-four of the Holy Rule. Chapter Two says: 'He holds the place of Christ.' No wonder the Rule repeats several times, 'Let the abbot always remember that at the fearful judgement of God, not only his teaching, but also his disciples' obedience will come under scrutiny.' 'The abbot should avoid all favouritism.' 'He must know what a difficult and demanding burden he has undertaken, directing souls and serving a variety of temperaments, coaxing, reproving and encouraging them as appropriate.' This is the burden of 'the care of souls'.

In chapter sixty-four St Benedict wrote of the abbot, 'His goal must be profit for the monks not pre-eminence for himself' . . . 'He must be chaste, temperate, merciful . . . hate faults but love the brothers . . . Let him strive to be loved rather than feared.' 'He must not be excitable, anxious, extreme, obstinate, jealous or over-suspicious.' 'Such a man is never at rest . . .' 'He should be discerning and moderate . . . so arrange everything that the strong have something to yearn for and the weak nothing to run from.'

The election of Father Basil to be abbot was daunting for him. Half of his community in the monastery, and most out on the parishes, called missions, were older 'in the habit' than he was. He was not only responsible in various ways for his 153 monks, but also for those under their care, some six hundred boys in the school, plus the parishioners in the considerable number of parishes served by the Ampleforth community, which extended from the local Yorkshire countryside through parts of Lancashire, Cumberland and South Wales, from Workington to Cardiff. Counting all the parishioners, the total 'community' under his care must have amounted to some thirty-five thousand souls. In addition, there was the dependent Priory of St Louis, Missouri, in the United States, founded from Ampleforth in 1955, which had its own associations, friends, schoolboys and parents, and to which, later, it was his privilege to grant independence.

Frenetic activity, over and above being father of his own monastic family, overtook Abbot Basil, as it seems to overtake many abbots. We can do little more here than list some of it. After the conclusion of the Vatican Council, renewal was in the air. He found himself member of the Benedictine Confederation's commission *de re monastica* (on monastic renewal); by 1973 he was chairman of that commission – which had meant considerable travel to Rome and to some European monasteries. It was on one of these journeys to Rome (1976) that Paul VI told him at a private meeting that as a good monk, he should accept the archbishopric of Westminster.

Whoever put up his name were not satisfied with his being voted on to the above commission of the Confederation, but at the 1970 General Meeting of the abbots of the world, he was elected to the commission on Ecumenism and made Chairman as well. His work in these areas could be another chapter.

Meanwhile he became a member of the committee of the GBA (the Governing Body of the Association of Independent Schools) and, a nice touch, a Governor of the great Jesuit school, Stonyhurst College, a long-standing rival and friendly establishment.

In 1973 he was the canonical visitor to the Abbey of Maredsous in Belgium. These and the business of granting independence to the Priory of St Louis, in the United States, demanded much travel, vast correspondence. Perhaps it was fortunate that the commission on Ecumenism lost two of the four original abbot members by resignation of their abbacies, thus leaving Abbot Basil in England and another abbot in distant Brazil, which brought that work to a halt.

As abbot he had to steady some of the community, especially during those wind-tossed years, who were finding monastic life extremely difficult. He would spend hours listening, encouraging, reassuring; even more hours going from one group to another, now in Cardiff, now in Lancashire or Cumberland, back to Ampleforth, on to St Benet's, Oxford. Likewise to him fell the necessity of breaking the sad news of a departure. Though not catastrophic these facts were very painful to all the members of a close-knit community, to him an hourly agony. Here is one way he introduced the matter to the Community:

> I have to give you, I am afraid, Fathers, bad news and probably the Community a bit of a shock. This is a source of great sadness to me and no doubt to you. You will not expect me to tell you the reasons which led to the decision of this particular Brother to leave us. I can best sum it up, I think, by saying that the heart had gone out of his vocation. And once that happens and a man becomes unsettled to the degree where the strain is too much, it seems only prudent to release him.

These departures were like so many deaths in the intimacy of the family, for that is what a monastery is, a spiritual family.

In those troubled times he had a way of deflating the tensions of the zealots, of the ideologues, by bringing up a subject – for example, of celibacy, poverty, work, choir – and admitting that he did not know all the answers. He knew some, but again was not quite satisfied with the reasons given. He was always a learner, always seeking – the essence of intellectual humility.

Neither the Community nor the outside world will know till doomsday the strains that Abbot Basil experienced in those years, or the full strength and power of the support he gave to his monks, which saved the traditions of the House at Ampleforth from disintegration. Something of his agony shows in the tension of the eyes and hands in that outstanding portrait of him by Derek Clark, which still hangs in the monastery refectory.

'Aggiornamento'

A monastery by its nature is conservative; it clings to its traditions, as it follows the Rule. An old Prior, Prior Bede Turner, used to intone 'no innovations' and that was that. With the advent of the Second Vatican Council and with that one word of the good Pope John, *aggiornamento*, the tempo throughout the Church was changed. The more traditional the situation, the more tumultuous the upsurge of novel ideas.

Becoming Abbot in 1963, Father Basil was faced by the need to come to terms with new ideas, to marry the new and the old. He had had, during his student years at Fribourg, more time to study, think and pray than most of his monks, so he had a clear advantage. Having been a member of the regular Meetings of the Regimen of the English Benedictine Congregation, even as a simple monk, since he was Delegate of the Ampleforth Community and Master of Monastic Studies, he was ahead of most of his brethren in his thinking about the Church's programme of monastic renewal. One of his clear duties was to coax his Community to undertake a steady re-think about their life: the timetable, the works they had undertaken, school and parishes, the Liturgy in the vernacular, the already revised texts of the Mass; the re-adjustment of values, spiritual, academic and social; of poverty and riches.

Abbot Basil used to say privately: 'I am sowing the seed and do not expect to see an immediate harvest.' New ideas take a long time to be assimilated. The shift in the Liturgy was the first to emerge, with tentative vernacular services; and the shift in works, with an increase of interest in retreats. During his abbacy, which lasted one term and a half, thirteen years in all, his aims included the following. He would bring the Liturgy to the people according to the suggestions of the Constitution on the Liturgy of Vatican II, *Sacrosanctum Concilium*, by introducing the language of the people into the Divine Office and the Mass, by adapting the times and quality of the Divine Office to the local needs, by introducing the study of the Liturgy for young monks, by allowing Communion in both kinds – providing all this was in tune with the mind of the Church.

He set up many discussions in the monastery and in the parishes to establish an understanding of the new needs of the People of God, and of how the Benedictine presence could best be expressed in pastoral ways. He was concerned that in the monastic schools there should be an examination of the ways of teaching boys religion in this increasingly pluralistic world from which they came and to which they would go back. He wanted an enquiry into other apostolic works at and around the Abbey and parishes; retreat centres (The Grange and Redcar); an active co-operation with the ecumenical movement.

The ecumenical direction given to Ampleforth during Father Basil's time as abbot was strong and effective. A network of links with the local churches, Anglican and Methodist, was created. The most long-lasting was what came to be known as 'The Abbot's Group', which still meets once a month. The blind and holy Vicar of Normanby, Father Gordon Thompson – now some years dead and in his last years Canon of York – must be honoured as co-founder. The group met to grasp the meaning of the thought of Vatican II, to study the different traditions of spirituality, to explore ways of co-operation at the local level.

Next in importance was the Ryedale Christian Council, one of the earliest in the country (1960), working at ecumenism at the grass roots. A similar Council was also encouraged, centred at Easingwild and embracing Stillington, Crayke and Gilling. A unique link was established with the Orthodox Churches when an Orthodox House was set up in Oswaldkirk (1½ miles away), where boys from any part of the Orthodox faith could live, sleep and pray, but join the boys of the School in studies, recreation and sport. St Symeon's House was a valuable witness to the desire for unity between East and West.

In his visits to other monastic houses, either when making a formal visitation or as a guest, he had many opportunities to observe the change of mores. Some saddened him. He saw a real problem, a dissipation of spirit, in the introduction of radios and television into the monastic houses; the search for *divertissement* to escape into triviality when God's work is pressing. Of course, in monastic life radio and television do have their limited uses, for occasional relaxation, for study, for an awareness of what is afoot in the world.

Looking back over Father Basil's years as abbot, what emerges is that for him it was the people, the monks who were primary. He could happily let others work on feasibility plans, but individual members of the Community, their material and especially their spiritual well-being, came first; and each monk was different, each required a different approach. They could not in one sense be treated equally. Some were weak, some strong.

He wanted deeper appreciation of the monastic life itself as witness in the world, witness to prayer, to obedience, to poverty, to humility, to chastity, and to community.

Much of this had to be an ongoing process, which could penetrate the whole Community, as such, very slowly. A great ship cannot change direction as fast as a skiff, nor can a church in one life's span. His phrase was: 'You can't swivel the Queen Mary round on a six-penny piece.' On the one hand monasteries had the middle-aged, who tended to cling to the rigidities of the 40s and 50s; the old who were young in spirit, or too old to protest; the young sometimes arrogantly certain about uncertainties, impatient at the slow pace of change, or spoiling to 'jump the gun'; a certain timidity in authority – what will Rome think? All this created a delicate 'political' situation. The picture in the dioceses and their parishes was not very different when later he came to know his own Archdiocese.

Abbot Basil came to realize more clearly, particularly in his second cut-short term of only four years, that programmes or elaborate schemes were not God's way. They were good as far as they went, but they did not go far enough, or rather, not deep enough. We, the People of God, including monastic communities, are just pilgrims, members of a Pilgrim Church, searching for God's way, waiting upon His will, trying to grasp the underlying divine reality beneath our not worthless, but limited, activities and plans. Prayer and contemplation is a primary need, particularly in the active regions of the Church's life. As Abbot Basil said:

> This should not lead to inactivity. We must grope on, but in great humility, and listening to God's own sign language. We must not become cynical, despising *all* activity, yet always stand back a little to see God's idea behind ours – trust and pray.

When we consider the staggering blows that hit the Religious Orders and individual monastic houses throughout the Church in the late sixties and early seventies of this century, after the close of the Second Vatican Council, we have to thank God, as a Community, that he gave us at Ampleforth such an Abbot at that crucial period. So that despite the defections, the hesitations and the confusions, Ampleforth had stability and remained at peace, and since that time has been able to build on that humbling and enlightening experience.

Something of all this shows through in Abbot Hume's book, *Searching for God*, which, it will be remembered, was drawn from the weekly talks to his monastic community. The book has integrity and simplicity, a Benedictine spirituality, one might almost dare to say, an Ampleforth spirituality.

Living in Community for Father Basil never meant the minimum of mutual toleration – which is scarcely human, let alone Christian. Community living meant caring, affection, appreciation, support, all of which came naturally to him. Of course the quirks of others got on his nerves, but not unduly. Those early years were the ones during which he learnt what he taught so well as Abbot. For example, in *Searching for God*, we find:

> The aspect of community life upon which I wish to reflect is . . . The emotional part, our affections; you must never be frightened of your affections. If you did not feel drawn to some persons more than to others, you would, I think, be a very odd person. Secondly, remember that you cannot ignore your emotions, as if they did not exist. Thirdly they cannot be stifled . . . They are part of you (pp. 44–5).

How to deal with them? He gives a simple, tentative, rule of thumb: say 'Yes' to others, and very often 'No' to oneself (p. 45). Speaking of celibacy which he sees as imitating Christ, he warns:

> It is not right to allow other people to fall in love with us . . . We have to be good human beings, warm and spontaneous in our relations with other people, but sane and sensible, recognizing our frailty (p. 47).

This sentence provides the necessary counter-balance to the earlier one. There is nothing learnt for learning's sake, nothing soft but nothing to crush the bruised soul, a virile approach to difficulties, Christian hope.

Thus when Father Basil came to Westminster he was not without pastoral and administrative experience in areas akin to those of a diocesan bishop. He was besides already in close touch with the English hierarchy because he was Superior of many parishes within their jurisdiction. They could already assess his worth, and he theirs, even before his appointment.

One surely should be permitted to end this chapter on a note of gratitude and confidence; be assured that his spirit as Abbot still pervades his subsequent career in the wider world.

3

A Benedictine Spirituality

Perhaps the oddest paradox of church life is the reluctance of many bishops and priests to act as spiritual guides. Odd, because if there is one thing the man in the street expects from the clergy it is the ability to speak with conviction and expert knowledge of the inner world of mind and heart and soul. As bankers are presumed to know about money matters, doctors about medicine, and generals about warfare, so bishops are presumed to understand the spiritual life. Yet many are ill-at-ease when cast in the role of, as they would describe it, 'spiritual guru'. They prefer to talk of diocesan finances, building programmes, parish administration, Catholic schools, vocations, ecclesiastical regulations, social or moral problems, anything in fact except the Christian's inner life as such. For that kind of thing, they imply, inquirers should turn to Religious or to diocesan priests with a reputation for being good spiritual directors. The motive for such coyness may not be discreditable; it may spring from natural diffidence or a genuine difficulty in finding words for an area of experience which is invisible and intangible, or an understandable distaste for the kind of self-revelation that the spiritual teacher finds virtually inescapable. But there it is. Bishops are frequently remembered as brilliant administrators or eloquent community spokesmen, or as scholars, or as pioneers of various good works; very few are remembered first and foremost as masters of the spiritual life.

It needs no remarkable insight to recognize that Cardinal Hume would wish to be included among that few. From his first days as Archbishop it was evident that his primary concern would be to nurture the inner life of those he had been called out of his monastery to serve. The message was unmistakable, not only in what he said but in what he was, in the striking initial impression he made not only on his Catholic community but on other religious believers, and even on many with no religious beliefs at all.

My own first glimpse of him was on the day of his ordination as bishop, from an eyrie high above the chancel where I was doing the radio commentary for the BBC. I cannot remember what I said. I do remember what I thought. He came up the aisle like a man taking a brisk country walk across open fields. He looked shy and somewhat overwhelmed by the enthusiasm of the congregation's welcome, but acknowledged it with a natural, unaffected friendliness and rather less natural, indeed stilted, gestures of blessing which at best looked awkwardly dutiful. Such details may seem pointless. But to see a man so unaffectedly himself on such an occasion was something of a shock. High office takes men in peculiar ways, and high ecclesiastical office is no exception. Latent inclinations to pomposity, vanity, artificiality, can be horridly exposed in the limelight and tension of public ceremonies. And as public ceremonies are integral to a churchman's life he consciously or unconsciously, according to temperament, his understanding of his office, and his reaction to what he believes is expected of him, falls into role-playing. Some adopt the mien of 'the prince of the Church', others 'the man of piety', others 'the father of the family', others 'the servant of his people'. Anyone used to church ceremonies quickly begins to distinguish the stereotypes, not necessarily in any unkindly spirit, but simply for what they are. Yet the danger of some element of falsity generating scepticism and undermining the relationship between pastor and people keeps winking through. Fellini detected it and guyed it unmercifully in his film '8½' where silken, practised bishops were caricatured as clothes-horses on roller skates, mechanically sketching hieratic gestures, empty of faith or conviction, on the surrounding air.

What surprised about Cardinal Hume was the absence of any trace of these familiar stereotypes. He was utterly and vulnerably himself, every feeling registering, from the wish to be anywhere but here, to the evident determination to fulfil his new office as best he could, however unpalatable it might be. By the time he reached the sanctuary steps a line from the Gospel was running unbidden through my mind: 'Behold a man in whom there is no guile.'

That highly subjective impression, reinforced though it was by the Cardinal's unwrought words spoken straight from the heart later in the ceremony, would be entirely worthless if it had been unique. But it was not. In the following days and weeks any amount of public and private comment centred on that same powerful impression; a quality of directness, of utter candour, of vulnerability. It was immensely attractive, it made for trust. I have laboured the point because it has much to do with the Cardinal's impact as a spiritual teacher. Unless I am hopelessly mistaken, it mainly explains his drawing-power, whether on television or radio, or through his writings, even among people who would not normally give their attentions to a priest. There are priests who talk fluently, even movingly, about the things of the spirit, but who leave a niggling impression that they are not genuinely in touch with what they describe. There are priests who talk about God as if they had dissected Him in a laboratory, yet who do not seem actually to know Him. The Cardinal is not an orator. He does not express himself memorably. The things he says are very simple and often very familiar. But they sound as if they had been kitchen-tested. He never seems to speak merely for effect. And when he talks about God he communicates a vivid sense that this God is absolutely real at least to him.

There is something else. And again an anecdote. My next opportunity to observe the new Cardinal was at rather closer quarters. The event was an informal dinner attended mainly by Catholic laymen from a cross-section of the professions, not much given to hero-worship and, though decently respectful, not inclined to be awed by churchmen however exalted in rank. Like myself, few had any previous acquaintance with the former abbot and there was much curiosity about what manner of man he was. Suddenly he was in the room, smiling and joking, a rather boyish figure despite his white hair and black Benedictine habit. And with him came the sense of another presence. My neighbour whispered to me, 'He's brought God into the room'. The remark may sound theatrical but it certainly summed up what the people in the room were thinking then and throughout the evening. And I have heard the same sentiment repeated, in various shapes and forms, many times since. Where the Cardinal is, to an unusual degree, he inspires a strong awareness of the reality and presence of God in others.

The ability to inspire that awareness is not unique, but it is uncommon. There are many terms which religious people use to distinguish those whom they feel have some special spiritual quality: a man of God, a man of faith, a man close to God – or, of course, a woman, as the case may be. But there is no adequate term for the rare few who seem to be accompanied by a second presence, a kind of shadow self which appears more real and imposes on the attention more powerfully than the flesh-and-blood human being it accompanies. This phenomenon is difficult to describe and baffling to experience. Yet the reaction to it is consistent. In the presence of such personalities people find themselves attending to, thinking about, God with unusual immediacy and concentration. It might be assumed that anyone professionally dedicated to religion would have that effect. In practice that is not the case. Quite a lot of bishops and priests attract much the same interest and attention, and invite much the same scrutiny, as might members of the royal family, politicians or other public personalities. And the thoughts they provoke can be much the same: 'They look kind/unkind, good-humoured/surly, reserved/affable, distinguished/unimpressive.' They may strike the onlooker as men of action or reflective men, as calm or nervy, as outgoing or inward-looking. Conversation is likely to turn on their diplomatic gifts or powers of leadership or their cast of mind. It is an exceptional personality who makes the presence of God impinge more powerfully than his own, who in some way reflects attention away from himself. The Cardinal possesses that gift – and gift, of course, it is.

Whatever its source, it does not imply a colourless personality. Cardinal Hume is not merely a walking signpost with no character of his own. On the contrary, the impact he makes as a man for whom the world of the spirit is absolutely real is reinforced by human qualities that have a general appeal. The British do not like their churchmen to be too ethereal, too detached from everyday reality, like figures in a holy picture. The Cardinal seems well-rooted in this world, with a liking, as well as a professional concern, for ordinary people, and a natural taste for everyday pleasures like music and sport. He talks simply and directly without clerical affectations. He admits endearingly to doubts and hesitations. He makes spontaneous jokes, often against himself. And in a nation besotted with sport, the fact that he played squash, and jogged, and followed Newcastle United, was a reassuring trait that probably caught the attention of agnostics more effectively than if he had raised the dead to life in the middle of Piccadilly Circus. At least among his countrymen the case for the world to come is not buttressed by an evident contempt for life in this world, here and now. The Cardinal's recognizable humanity, far from detracting from his role as spiritual mentor, gains him a wider hearing. Certainly there is no smack of the hearty 'Look, I'm more worldly than you are' clergyman about him. But it is a fallacy to suppose that where spiritual matters are concerned people have more confidence in those who have failed to come to terms with, and lack relish for, the world around us and our present mortal life. On the contrary. They are more likely to be impressed when someone who evidently thinks this world is a good place to be, still insists that the world of the spirit is even more real and of even greater importance.

The Cardinal's authority as a spiritual leader rests then, first on his ability to make God real to his hearers, and secondly on a natural personality with broad appeal to his fellow countrymen and inviting their confidence. Two less obvious factors strengthen this relationship. The Cardinal is a Benedictine. And of all spiritual traditions the Benedictine is almost certainly the one most naturally in tune with the British, especially the English, temperament. Perhaps it would be even truer to say that the Benedictine tradition has been the matrix of that temperament. Before the Reformation it was the dominant tradition in the development of English spirituality. And in subtle ways it filtered into and left a stamp on the character of the Anglican Church after the breach with Rome. It is a tradition that nurtures a deep, single-minded attachment to the person of Jesus Christ but shrinks from theatrical or histrionic expressions of devotion and from fanatic expressions of faith. It is difficult to imagine a Benedictine standing by the Inquisitor's fire, or taking part in a procession of flagellants through Seville. Its watchword is Peace, and there is a vein of moderation, of proportion, of good sense, running through Benedictine spiritual teaching that discourages extremes of outlook or behaviour. It does not try to jettison human qualities but to harness them. It does not spend its energies on trying to build and furnish outlandish environments as far removed from, and as strikingly in contrast to, the world of man and nature as possible; rather with a touch here and a touch there it extends the natural into the supernatural, it reveals and draws out the invisible divine presence within the visible human world. It does not try to recast human nature but to complete it. It does not fling itself headlong against the *civitas mundi* with fire and sword, but seeks to penetrate it and convert it from within. It does not loathe and scorn the broad range of human activity but is profoundly respectful of its character, its achievements, and its complexity. There are other traditions, other approaches, to spirituality, both within the Catholic Church and outside it; the Benedictine tradition is well on the side of the incarnational, that spirituality which takes as its starting point the Word made Flesh. Christ came not to eradicate human nature or to obliterate the fields of human activity, but to purify and exalt them.

The tradition has other features almost as important. One of its key phrases is 'to seek'. The spiritual life is a process of exploration; it cannot be defined in a few simple lines, or neatly packaged in a few simple prescriptions. Within broad bounds everyone will find his own path, travel at his own speed and meet with varied experiences. True, there are general principles, everyone has the same map in his head. But the terrain can be covered and the goal reached by a great variety of personal routes. In turn this belief fosters a sensitive regard for differences of personality. Within a Benedictine community the skill of the Abbot lies in reading those differences and making allowances for them. He is there to foster unity of mind and heart among contrasting individuals, not to impose uniformity or to breed indistinguishable clones. They will have a common purpose but serve it through a wealth of individual interests and talents. Some will progress quickly, others at a slower pace. Some will need goading, others a check on the reins. Some will need indulgence, others respond better if they meet resistance. Some will thrive on encouragement, others sometimes require taking down a peg. It is a tradition uneasy with dogmatism and regimentation.

The Cardinal has been formed in that tradition and speaks out of it. He is a Benedictine monk and he has been a Benedictine abbot. He has not only lived by the Rule of St Benedict himself, he has interpreted it for his fellow monks. Unlike most churchmen, he has actually been elected to that office; and unlike most politicians, elected by people who have lived for years in the same community and know him very well. He has been chosen, therefore, by people in a good position to know, as someone especially exemplifying Benedict's ideals and unusually good at interpreting his mind. And it is therefore no surprise to recognize that the primacy he gives to the inner life, and his whole approach to spirituality, reflects the Benedictine tradition. To say also that it is his strength as a spiritual mentor, seriously attended to by many people outside his own communion as well as within it, and perhaps the explanation of an approach to other issues and areas of life which, at least from some quarters, attracts occasional criticism. The core of his spiritual teaching is by no means unconventional. It does not have the idiosyncratic stamp of a Ruysbroek or an à Kempis; still less is the Cardinal a guru figure like the Maharishi. What he has to say about the nature and means of holiness is familiar Catholic orthodoxy. It is the tone of voice which sets him apart from many, though by no means all, Catholic bishops who, when all is boiled down, are saying much the same things. Through his sermons, writings and speeches there is an acute sensitivity to the differences of character, experience and circumstance among those he is addressing. Church leaders can sometimes sound like regimental sergeant-majors, or instructors putting commandoes over an obstacle course. There is no room for laggards or the fainthearted. The Cardinal makes room for both, and tempers the wind to the shorn lamb. Nor does this sound like a calculated tactic. He shows unusual respect for individual experience, not least for individual difficulties. Even more unusually he speaks to those finding the going rough and the way uncertain, as one who has shared that experience and found that by pressing on the going gets better and light returns. There is a depth of sympathy here which is touching as well as persuasive. It does not mean watering down ideals or fudging principles. But better, he seems to say, to go an inch in the right direction if that is all you can manage, than to abandon the journey because a mile seems too far. You, he says, may feel yourself a failure. But only God can really judge failure – and one of our surest convictions about God is that He is merciful.

To be an encourager, to be an enfolder rather than an excluder, to make allowances for individual strengths and weaknesses, is a fundamental strength of the spiritual guide. It has much to do with the fact that when he speaks on the spiritual life the Cardinal inspires confidence and is heard attentively. He strengthens faith, he puts fresh heart into his hearers. The same breadth of sympathy is not always, however, so effective in other areas where people look to him for guidance. In matters of public controversy, whether political or ecclesiastical, he often speaks more guardedly than those with emphatic views on one side or the other would wish. This may be the result of personal temperament; as an abbot he was sometimes accused of being indecisive. It may be no more than a decent respect for the complexity of situations where there may be something to be said for both, or several, sides of an argument. But it is not entirely impossible that the same instinct which makes him a good spiritual mentor is at work in this other role; that he is always looking for the good that can be built on, the elements that deserve encouragement, grounds for reconciliation between contending parties. Sometimes this approach can be read as an attempt to square the circle. It can disappoint and exasperate those who have reached firm conclusions or who nurse firm convictions, whether conservatives in religious matters or radicals in social matters. It does not march well with a public world which argues in strident slogans. But at a deep level it may get results from politicians and fellow churchmen which no amount of scolding and denunciation would achieve. Even if the Cardinal may miss the chance from time to time, as his critics contend, to give a firm lead on issues where in practical life sides have to be taken, in the long run his attempt to reach through to the private person behind the public role, to the best instincts in all, may prove the wiser course. It certainly adds force to his words on the relatively infrequent occasions when he makes a strong statement on some public issue.

As well as being a Benedictine the Cardinal is, it has to be remembered, half-French. It is easy to overlook the fact, given his quintessentially English manner and interests. But, coming through his mother, French spirituality, the most subtle and profound in Western Christendom, must have influenced his faith from a very early age. The French have produced so many great masters of the spiritual life. They have charted the movements of the spirit, probed the psychology of faith, made a science of spiritual development and growth. They intimately link spirituality and theology – which may seem obvious but cannot always be taken for granted. Within that tradition French Catholics often speak about the interior life without embarrassment, and with a fluency and precision unusual elsewhere. Yet acutely sensitive though it is to the invisible order, and aware of spiritual possibilities, that tradition is also hard-headed, disciplined, deeply rooted in everyday reality. It has nothing in common with a number of fashionable spiritual cults which are little more than a disguised ego-trip. It is God-attentive, an orderly exercise which seeks to shift the centre of interior awareness from what Iris Murdoch once called 'the fat relentless ego' to God and His immediate presence. To grow up in contact with that tradition, as well as the equally pragmatic but more reticent, private, less analytical English spirituality, with its stress on ardent individual devotion to the person of Christ and its curious strain of idiosyncratic mysticism, must have been a considerable enrichment. From both traditions the Cardinal would learn to take the development of the interior life for granted, a perfectly normal, and indeed the primary, activity for average people, not at all a high-falutin' specialized interest for a rarified minority. There is no need to look further to explain the vein of pragmatism in all that he says, or his assumption that the cultivation of the interior life lies within the capacity of all.

In two other respects, the experience of growing up as the child of a mixed marriage and moulded by two cultures, appears to have affected the Cardinal's outlook. One is his active interest in what is now called ecumenism, which ante-dated the Second Vatican Council, the other his regard for the European dimension of English Catholicism and national life. However understandable in the light of their painful history, until very recently English Catholics nursed an animosity, even a contempt, for their fellow Christians, especially the Established Church. And long years of stubborn self-reliance had developed a certain complacency and attendant suspicion of 'the Church on the continent'. Bishops and priests were given to boasting of the superior virtues of Catholics in Britain compared with continental Catholics, and to insisting that the local church had 'nothing to learn from those foreigners'. The Second Vatican Council shattered this complacency once and for all. Yet in the case of Cardinal Hume he has never appeared to share either prejudice, but from very early days to have looked for ways of improving relations with other Christians and strengthening links with fellow Catholics on the European mainland. That too broadens his appeal as a spiritual leader. It would be hard to find in his sermons and addresses any trace of that jarring arrogance, or what might be called chauvinist Catholicism, which has so often stopped the ears of people at home and abroad to English Catholic leaders.

Although the Cardinal's personal qualities make so strong an impression on his hearers – and whether preaching, giving spiritual conferences, speaking on television or to small intimate groups of people, his directness and clarity grip the attention – transferred to the written page his words are not so compelling. He is not a phrase-maker. He does not share the prophetic fire of a Helder Camara or the rhetorical gifts of a Suenens or a John Paul II. He does not excite the imagination or stir doctrinal speculation. He sticks to main thoroughfares, with few excursions into the by-ways and alleys of popular devotion, esoteric piety and mystical theory. What concerns him are the great events of Christ's work of redemption, their meaning and their annual liturgical celebration; the great irrigation systems of the spiritual life – Prayer, the Eucharist, the Sacraments; the fundamental values on which a Christian way of life should be based; and he reads from a well-worn map familiar to generations of Catholics. He speaks plainly and simply. This may be a matter of temperament, or the result of his experience in the classroom, where matters have to be 'got across' in plain, orderly terms. There is certainly a textbook flavour to all his published writings. Their lucidity and simplicity, as well as the absence of sectarian embroidery, make them, however, accessible to most mainstream Christians not only to Catholics.

Such an account may make his writings sound, perhaps, too cut-and-dried, even mechanical: 'Follow the drill, and results are assured.' But that is not their effect. First, because there is a vein of scrupulous regard for the differences of outlook, experience and circumstances of life among his audience, and he never implies that precisely the same prescription will do for all. Second, because the rare but key images he employs belie any notion that he views the spiritual life in static terms. The dominant image – it finds its way into the titles of both his published books as well as recurring throughout the text – is that of the wayfarer, or, in religious terms, the pilgrim. To the Cardinal, man is by nature a seeker, one who consciously or unconsciously hungers for meaning and happiness; and in his own words 'the search for meaning and the search for happiness are a single search'. Man has a destiny, and, consciously or unconsciously, he travels towards that destiny which, whether he knows it or not, is an appointment with God. Man is incomplete and hungers for completeness, though the completeness he desires lies outside the scope of his own natural powers:

> There is a need today in every profession and walk of life to rediscover a sense of purpose. I speak of an ultimate purpose that makes sense, that is one which corresponds to man's deepest aspirations and needs, or rather fulfils them.

The one who satisfies that need, offers that fulfilment, is God; and, the Cardinal adds: 'I believe that the yearning for God is becoming more and more intense.'

The Christian shares this fundamental human hunger. But for him the goal of his pilgrimage is at least adumbrated, he has a guide, Christ Himself, a caravan of fellow pilgrims to travel with, a map and compass, and special resources for his journey. The Cardinal does not suggest that the Christian way to God is the only way, but that it is the tried and trusted way opened up and made known to the human family through God Incarnate.

This image, which implies movement and discovery, and in the Cardinal's usage relationships also, undermines any assumption that the spiritual life is merely a matter of set routine from cradle to grave. So too does another charming, less classical image, his description of the relationship between the human spirit and God as a game of hide-and-seek. This brings out the fact that man's search for God is not one-sided but almost a kind of dance, in which God is no less anxious to reveal Himself and embrace His human children than they to penetrate the world of the invisible and to take hold of God. In both images there is the sense of progress by stages, of discovery in glimpses, of fulfilment by degrees. The spiritual life involves hard going, darkness broken only by occasional gleams of light, uncertainty only occasionally relieved by moments of reassurance. It is here that the Cardinal appears to speak out of personal experience and as one who has travelled this way himself. He is beckoning, not pointing, telling of lived reality, not of some academic theory.

Personal experience may lie also behind the warm and appealing terms in which he speaks of God, the end of our journeying. 'We must never fail to trust in the love of God', he insists, 'to have confidence that He wants our good.' The main difficulty for the spiritual pilgrim is to accept the reality of that love, to grasp it as a living truth not just a pious platitude:

> It is harder for many people to believe that God loves them than to believe that He exists . . . We learn the power and the urgency of this love of God by looking at the actions and attitudes of His Divine Son.

It is to the gospels that the Cardinal turns to find firm grounds for that difficult conviction. And especially when with beguiling simplicity he draws out the tremendous implications of three related parables, those of the lost coin, the lost sheep, and the lost son, in the fifteenth chapter of St Luke. There, he says, we are able to look directly into God's inner nature and His attitude to each and every human creature. That is the bedrock of Christian faith, the motive and source of energy for the human pilgrimage. And in real life, in history, that inner nature finds its ultimate, most eloquent expression, in the figure of Christ dying on the cross. That is where we see how much man matters to God, that is how we can be confident that our belief in His love, His mercy, His forgiveness, is no illusion.

All else on man's side is a response to that love. The whole of the spiritual life is a prolonged effort to love God in return. And here the Cardinal does indeed see a place for habit and routine, as there is a place for them in the growth of human relationships. Romantic feeling, pious sentiment, will not sustain the spiritual life over the long haul, any better that they are likely to support a lifelong human relationship such as marriage. The business has to be worked at, and there are no short cuts to success. In the Cardinal's view spiritual development needs 'stickability', perseverance in a steady routine of practices, adapted to and varying from one individual to another, but in all cases independent of shifts of mood and feeling. Whether he is talking about prayer, or the place of the Eucharist and the Sacraments in the Christian's everyday life, his advice is down-to-earth, practical, specific. His advice, for example, to say a prayer when going through a particular door in one's house catches this attention to detail exactly. But there is an even deeper reason for this emphasis on routine. Whenever he looks for counsel or motivation, the spiritual pilgrim can take only so much on trust. For the most part he must make his own discoveries. And he does so, in the old army slogan, by keeping on keeping on. The inner meaning, the value, the effects of prayer can only be learned by praying. So too with the Eucharist. So too with other elements of the Christian way of life, such as the practice of self-denial. We learn by doing.

One question remains. Is the spiritual life, then, simply a private, individual matter, with any kind of social concern or obligation tacked on as an optional extra? The Cardinal emphatically does not take that view. Among people experienced in spiritual direction it is widely held that the individual interior life can develop from active involvement in works of charity and justice, or it can develop first and then overflow into such activities; but whatever the starting-point, both elements are necessary for a full Christian life. On balance the Cardinal seems to think most naturally in terms of the second kind of development, from the inner life to concern for the outer world, but not at the expense of social involvement. There are echoes of the balance he has in mind when he discusses the role of the Church in politics:

> The Church can never be the servant of an ideology, or of a political system, nor can she be exclusively concerned with the next world . . . She is principally concerned with 'the truth concerning man'.

No less is the individual to act in and for this world as well as to have regard for the next. To achieve full humanity the whole man must be engaged. The spiritual life is not just an individualistic self-improvement scheme, a preoccupation with one's own soul. It has an essential social dimension, it is nourished by the wisdom and within the comradeship of the Christian community. Its vitality and genuineness can be outwardly gauged by effective love of the neighbour. The relationship is neatly expressed in a few lines of reflection on the Resurrection:

> It is important for ourselves and our society that we retain and develop a sane and wholesome faith, a sense of the eternal and the spiritual, a set of values and attitudes that will respect human dignity and shape a more human society.

That is, perhaps, not a bad note on which to conclude. Different people, different groups pin a variety of expectations on church leaders. From the very first Cardinal

Hume has planted a flag showing where he stands. The encouragement of a 'sane and wholesome faith' a 'sane and wholesome spirituality' is his chief preoccupation as a church leader. Not only as the way to that meaning and happiness for which each human spirit longs, but as the foundation of 'a sane and wholesome society'. It is a calm and steadying message for an often frenetic world.

4

Archbishop and Pastoral Leader

How can the pastoral work of a bishop be evaluated? It must, I suggest, be examined within the framework of two dimensions – Renewal and Mission. Renewal is concerned not with the shoring up of a dilapidated and crumbling structure and organization (which is one way of looking at maintenance), but with the building up of an organism – the development of the Body of Christ, the Church, and of life in each of its members. Mission is concerned with alerting those members of the Church to recognize their role as instruments shaped and prompted by God to fulfil His purposes.

The Scriptural anchorage for the first could be St Paul's expression of it to the Galatians: 'For my children you are, and I am in travail with you over again until I see Christ formed in you' (Galatians 4:19). That powerful image of a mother bringing her child into the world, with all the pains and joys associated with childbearing, is one that the father of a diocese must always have in mind.

The Scripture basis for Mission is that laid down for the Christ in the prophecy of Isaiah and taken up by Jesus as His manifesto in St Luke's gospel:

> The Spirit of the Lord is upon me because he has anointed me; he has sent me to announce good news to the poor, to proclaim relief for prisoners and recovery of sight for the blind, to let the broken

victims go free, to proclaim the year of the Lord's favour (Luke 4:18).

The theological reflection on the first is to be found in the Second Vatican Council document *Lumen Gentium*, which looks at the nature of the Church, what it is and what are its parts. The theological reflection on the mandate of Christ passed on to His disciples is to be found in another Second Vatican Council document *Gaudium et Spes*, known in English as *The Church in the World Today*. Anyone with responsibility in the Church must examine his work in the light of these Scriptural and Church statements.

The Vatican Council document on the Church sketched out the nature and role of the episcopacy, but for its practical application we must turn to the same Council's Decree on the Pastoral Role of Bishops. A key phrase at the beginning of the Decree, which indicates why it is necessary to take a closer look at the pastoral office of bishops, at the same time hints that it could never be the last word on the subject. 'Attentive to the development in human relations which has brought about a new order of things in our time', the Second Vatican Council saw how necessary it was for a bishop to recognize what was happening in the world about him, and to learn from that to widen and deepen his vision if he was to be faithful to the work handed on to him through the Apostles.

The burden of this Decree is that a bishop has to be a good pastor (in the Scriptural tradition of the Good Shepherd, seen in the Father and in Jesus); he has also to be a good servant in the pattern of the Anointed One – the Christ – anointed for service both to His Father and to the whole of creation.

The Decree on the Pastoral Role of Bishops is all about relationships. As one commentator puts it, 'the Decree succeeds in returning the Episcopacy to its original vocation in the Church while closing the gap now existing between

George Hume's parents, William and Marie ("Mimi")

An early photograph of the young George.

Hume, a keen rugger player, in his college's first XV.

With his father in Ampleforth village.

At a festival for young people in Glastonbury.

The Cardinal in his Benedictine habit, outside Westminster Cathedral.

With Archbishop Derek Worlock of Liverpool.

An ecumenical gathering of church leaders that includes Dr Runcie, Archbishop of Canterbury, and the Reverend Gordon Barritt, President of the Methodist Conference.

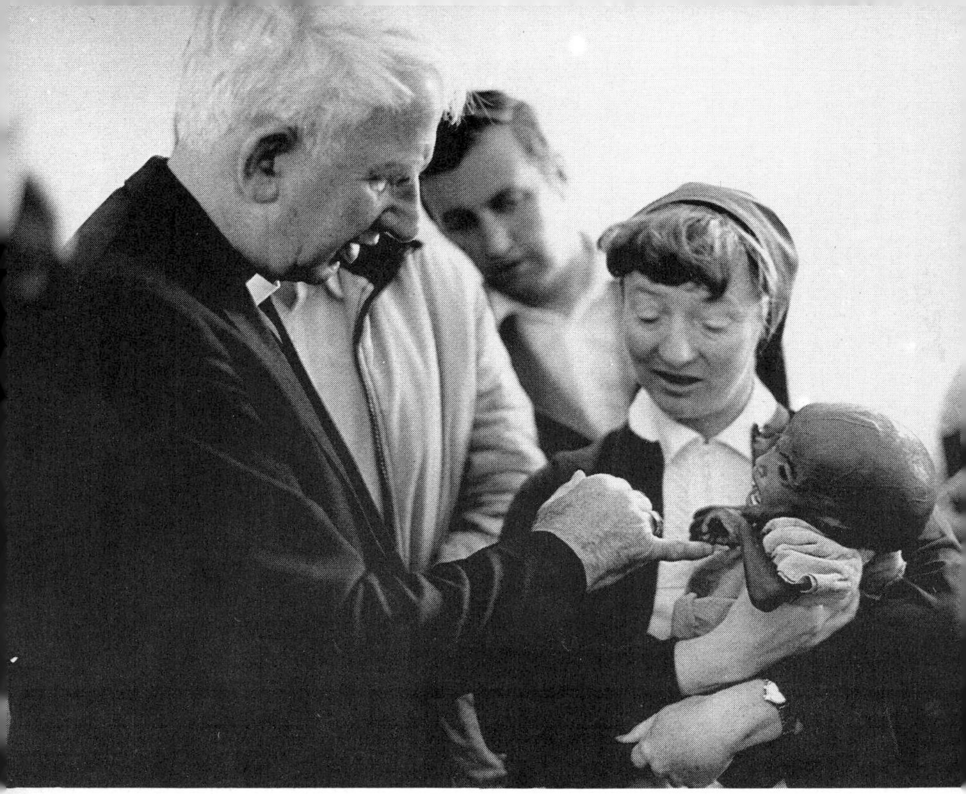

November 1984: the Cardinal's visit to Ethiopia – a clinic in Makalle.

A warm greeting for a victim of the Ethiopian disasters.

Meeting a young member of the Community after a Mass to celebrate the Dominican centenary.

With a patient at St Joseph's Hospice.

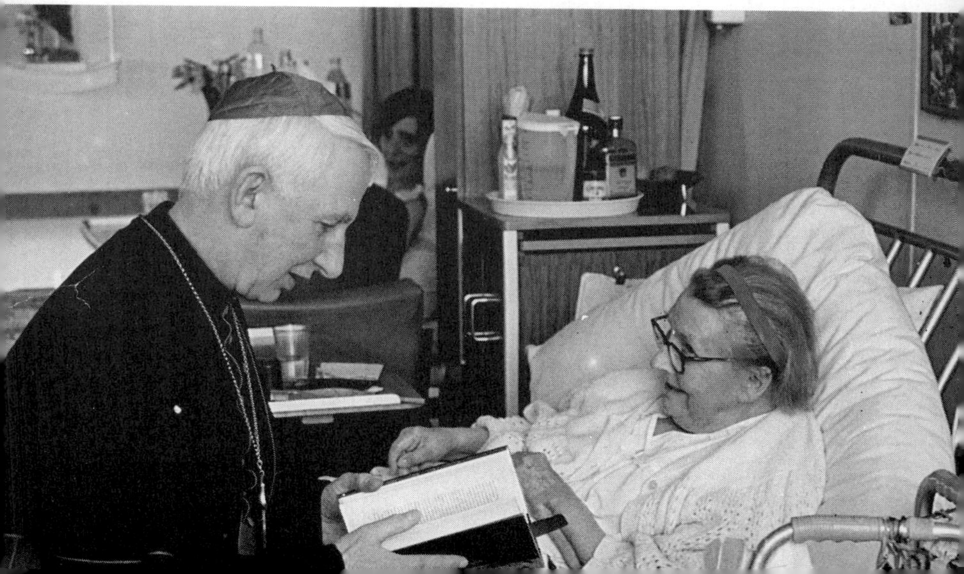

Archbishop and Cardinal: a pilgrimage to Walsingham, the shrine revered by Anglicans and Roman Catholics alike.

25th March 1976: George Basil Hume is ordained Bishop and installed as Archbishop of Westminster.

The new Archbishop waves a greeting after his installation.

Bishops, Clergy and Laity, through a new dedication to the teaching, evangelizing, and pastoral office of Bishops!'

Twenty years on and here in England (with the constantly changing 'new order of things' in mind) a more updated yardstick for the measuring of episcopal achievement or failure must be the Liverpool Congress Report. In 1980 this voiced the needs of the Church in this country and marked out the areas calling for urgent pastoral concern. These are expressed in the seven sector reports of the Congress:

1. The People of God – co-responsibility and relationship
2. The People of God – ministry, vocation, apostolate
3. Marriage and Family
4. Evangelization
5. Christian education and formation
6. Christian witness
7. Justice

It would be reasonable and fair to evaluate the last ten years of the pastoral work done in Westminster with those headings in mind.

One of the problems faced by the Second Vatican Council was the size of dioceses. Bishops must be able to carry out their pastoral duties effectively, and the size of most dioceses make this effectiveness very thin indeed. One of the means suggested to overcome this was the creation of smaller dioceses. Another was 'to divide existing dioceses with a new internal organization, especially when they are composed of rather large cities.'

Basil Hume became Archbishop of Westminster in March 1976. He came fully aware of the impossibility of the task before him as Bishop of the Diocese of Westminster, unless he shared his pastoral responsibilities by widespread delegation.

Within a few months was published *Planning for the Spirit*, which mapped out the reorganization of the diocese into five areas: Hertfordshire, Central, Western, Northern and Eastern London, each area consisting of some forty-five parishes. The number of Auxiliary Bishops in the diocese was increased to five, and the areas were entrusted to their care. It was an entirely new kind of structure in which the Cardinal delegated pastoral responsibility to the Area Bishops, without abdicating his own final authority. 'The Diocese remains one Diocese, but each of the five areas will enjoy a large measure of autonomy.' The creation of pastoral areas was a legal fiction which depended for its effectiveness on the ability of the Cardinal to delegate authority, and to trust the good sense and pastoral drive of the bishops concerned.

The two reasons given for the reorganization were to enable the local community to be in closer contact with the bishop, and to involve more people in the life of the Church.

As the Cardinal wrote when he introduced the reorganization:

> I have borne in mind . . . our prime aim: to bring all men and women closer to Christ and to one another. We are concerned with spreading the good news of the Gospel, with making everyone enthusiastic for Christ and His work, with seeking ways to be sensitive to the prompting of the Holy Spirit. These are things which we must do together, helping and counselling each other in true charity.

Planning for the Spirit initiated an exercise in co-responsibility and relationship that involved not just the bishops and priests but every man and woman in the diocese.

After the publication of this document the pastoral work of the diocese fell into two levels: that of the Cardinal using centralized services to shape policies for the whole diocese;

and that of the Area Bishops implementing these policies and forming their own specific pastoral plans.

When Cardinal Hume came to Westminster he found already in existence many of the aids to full Christian life that the Liverpool Congress was later to ask for. The Marriage Tribunal of the Diocese, and its increasing pastoral work in the care of married life, enjoyed a worldwide reputation for efficiency. St Joseph's Centre for the handicapped, at Hendon, with its provision for the catechesis of the mentally handicapped was even then said to be the most advanced in Europe.

A constant cry from each of the Liverpool Congress sectors was to be for Christian formation and education. The Cardinal, on his arrival, found six major centres of formation in Westminster: All Saints Pastoral Centre at London Colney in Hertfordshire, a residential Centre for eighty participants; the Westminster Adult Religious Education Centre, which aimed to ensure that the understanding of the Faith in Adult Catholics was kept up to date with developments in theology and the contemporary world; the Centre for Parish Catechetics, based upon the RCIA (Rite for the Christian Initiation of Adults), for the training of catechists mainly concerned with those seeking membership of the Church and with preparation for the Sacraments and the involvement of parents in that process; the Westminster Religious Education Centre concerned with religious education and pastoral care of teachers in schools. (These strong servicing agencies, together with the Youth Service, are now united in the Westminster Diocesan Education Service.)

Two other centres are Cornerstone, which (at the Cathedral Conference Centre) provides opportunities to study the Christian faith in an atmosphere of prayer and community; and the St Thomas More Centre for Pastoral Liturgy at Manor House.

To these have been added, in the last ten years, the

Agency for Social and Pastoral Action (SPA) which was a direct response to the Congress. The aim of SPA is to stimulate and co-ordinate the social involvement of the Church at a diocesan level and at the area, deanery and parish levels. One of the key concepts of the programme is to emphasize that, apart from some necessarily specialized resource centres and services (e.g. for the handicapped and the deaf), charity is exercised at the parish and community level. A second concept is the essential responsibility of lay women and men for the social involvement of the Church. A third concept is the necessity of addressing causes as well as effects.

Out of the SPA group new initiatives are constantly growing – not surprising in view of growing material poverty and marginalization of many groups. Recent departments have been formed to deal with issues like unemployment, housing, and drugs. While preserving its own unique witness as the Church of the poor, the diocese is conscious that it must increase its partnership with the State. SPA enables it to have a permanent liaison group with the Church of England and other ecumenical bodies engaged in the same fields.

These diocesan agencies have enabled the dialogue between all those who make up the people of God (bishops, priests and laity), to grow healthily. At the diocesan level this can be seen in a series of conferences held at London Colney. The first, in 1980, drew together for a weekend the 250 delegates who had been preparing in their episcopal areas for the Liverpool Congress, and who met to coordinate Westminster's contribution to that national conference.

After Liverpool there was a firm determination that the initiatives launched there should not be lost in the diocese, and that the process of renewal it hoped for should be realized. A further Diocesan Conference was therefore convened by the Cardinal in January 1981, to examine ways in which the diocese could give flesh to the bones of the Liverpool Congress. These conferences provided bishops, priests and laity with a heartening experience of the Church in prayer and action, which it was felt should become a regular feature of the life of the diocese.

Cardinal Hume, out of whose initiative these conferences grew, directed that (to safeguard against the building up of an élite in the diocese) the opportunity of attendance should be extended to new members each year, to give as many as possible a personal experience of the diocese in prayer and action.

Directly related to these first experiences was the recommendation made at a meeting of the Cardinal and his area bishops in April 1981. It is an example of what is often produced at these think-tank meetings:

> The ultimate pastoral objective of the Diocese of Westminster is Evangelization, through PRAYER, FAITH and ACTION: By Prayer is meant the spiritual renewal of people through Prayer and the Sacraments; by Faith is meant the teaching and nourishing of people's faith; by Action is meant social welfare and care.

In 1982 the theme of the Diocesan Conference was 'Justice and Social Welfare', i.e. justice in the local community and the implications of being a Christian in the world today. In 1983 'Catechesis in our time' asked how faith could or should be passed on. In 1984 the theme was 'The Parish', with its emphasis on community seen in the Eucharist and other shared parochial activities. In 1985 the theme was 'The Role and Mission of Youth'; it sought to help young people, who were the main participants, to clarify their needs in the Church and the ways in which they can find their mission to the Church and to the world.

The principle behind all these conferences was not to produce an overall plan for the whole diocese, but to enable each of the pastoral areas to work out their own priorities in response to the Church's cry for help heard at the Liverpool Congress, and in the knowledge of the special needs of their own locality.

The dialogue and formation flowing from the central services of the diocese are paralleled within each of the areas, where the response to the Congress call for continuing formation and for the building up of community is best seen. In every field of work the involvement of non-ordained women and men is seen as a prerequisite to growth and mission. Within the pastoral areas of the diocese the involvement of lay people in the work of the Church has increased considerably. Several of the Area Bishops have lay men or women as Pastoral Assistants – whose tasks are to co-ordinate and organize meetings and programmes.

Examples of what is happening in some of the areas will give an idea of the kind of growth that becomes possible after such a decision as that taken in *Planning for the Spirit*.

As a result of de-centralization each area has its own team of lay pastoral workers centred on an area base and drawing upon the resources offered by the central agencies. The teams consist of nonordained men and women (on full- or part-time work) with responsibility for Adult Religious Education, Parish Catechetics, School Education, Youth, Prayer and Bible Groups, Social and Pastoral Action, the Handicapped, the Deaf. The make up of the teams varies from area to area, since they are dependent entirely upon the needs of the people within the areas. These needs express themselves through Parish and Deanery Councils (where these exist), but particularly through Area Assemblies and Conference weekends.

In his introduction to 'Planning for the Spirit' the Cardinal wrote:

> The number of persons devoted to the service of Christ in the Diocese, Priests, Religious and Laity,

> is impressive. We want to involve more, especially the young, in the work of evangelization which is the responsibility of each of us in virtue of our Baptism.

The work of the Pastoral Teams has been precisely that – to help people to grasp the full meaning of their life in Christ, that while they need Christ to fill out their lives, Christ needs them to fulfil His mission.

An essential element in the various pastoral plans that have evolved in the areas, has been the training of non-ordained men and women to accept responsibility and to recognize the ministries (in the Church as well as in the world) to which they are called by their baptism. In one area alone, as a result of a massive team enterprise of priests, lay women and men, programmes of discussion papers centred on Prayer, Scripture, and an application of these to present-day life (on the See, Judge and Act principle), resulted in the creation of courses for the training of some two hundred and fifty lay people in the skills of group leadership.

Leaders who have the talent and commitment to inspire parish and other catechetical groups are the driving force behind much of the renewal in our parishes. The Pastoral Team parish-catechetics worker trains and supports catechists drawn from the parishes to prepare young people for the Sacraments. This includes adult catechesis of the parents as sponsors of their children, and helps to form the parish as a faith community. Such leaders (and others in the parish community) need theological training, and much pioneer work is done here by the Adult Religious Education worker, in setting up courses of very high quality. In the work of catechesis, Religious Sisters have shown themselves to be a source of great strength and have successfully attracted young people into the work.

The work of renewal taking place in the parishes has resulted in an increase in the understanding of, and growth in, ministry – the service to which Christians are called by their baptism. While most of these ministries are concerned with our own evangelization (e.g. catechists), or with involvement in the Liturgy (Readers, extra-ordinary ministers of the Eucharist), the sense of the ministry we owe to the world is growing particularly in the fields of justice, peace and caring.

The promotion of the idea of co-responsibility in the Church has not been easy. The greatest obstacle is a doctrinal one – a misunderstanding of the nature of the Church. For the majority of Catholics the only acceptable model of the Church has been the institutional, hierarchical model. For these the model of a pilgrim Church or that of the Whole Christ, is difficult to accept. The pastoral implications of such models are blocked by previous education and experience. Not only are clergy reluctant to allow lay people due responsibility; lay people themselves will often still rely overmuch on the clergy and consequently be unwilling to intrude on what they consider to be the role of the priest. Only in recent years have lay people and priests (and this will include bishops) begun to be trained in the delicate courtesies of sharing responsibilities in the Church. And we have still a long way to go.

The work of Pastoral Teams could be destroyed by the lack of understanding of any unco-operative priest of the parish, and the consequent lack of enthusiasm of the parishioners who depend upon him for guidance.

For this reason, in one area 'Bishops-and-Priests Away-weeks' take place every eighteen months. Every priest engaged in pastoral work in the area is expected to spend a week together with the bishop and his fellow priests at the Diocesan Pastoral Centre. On the first occasion it was to look closely at their own understanding of the nature of the Church, where bishops and priests could share together their own difficulties in the variation of their accepted roles in the Church. On subsequent Away-weeks they have examined together the role of the laity as seen in Scripture and in the documents of the Church since Vatican II, and the relationship that must exist between priests and people to encourage responsible partnership between them in the service of God and of the world. This reflection together on the nature of the Church and the mutual support it gives, in both the process of learning and that of unlearning, is important if the work of renewal is to reach every part of the Church in the diocese. Whatever Pastoral Plans or Conferences or Progammes of renewal may be forged at diocesan or area level, the labour of seeding, planting and eventual harvesting, can only take place in the parishes or other groupings of Christians. 'The Bishop's principal relationship must be with his priests who are "fellow workers" of the Bishop' states the Decree on Bishops. One of the principal effects of the division of the diocese into areas has been to bring bishops and priests closer together. This is notable especially among the bishops themselves.

While each of the Area Bishops enjoys considerable autonomy in the running of his own area, they all recognize and value highly their relationship with the Cardinal and each other. While the Bishops meet together with the Cardinal once a fortnight in the Council of Diocesan Administration, they meet for one evening a month specifically to share pastoral concern. At least three times a year the Cardinal and Area Bishops spend a full two days together at a quiet house in the country, where they can tease out pastoral problems, and help each other to recognize and respond to any new need. I think it is true to say that every new venture of the last ten years has grown out of seeds sown in these days spent together.

The division into areas has enabled bishops to know their priests and their people better. Having only forty-five or so parishes in his care, the Area Bishop is freer to spend more time with his priests. Each area has its Deans' group (four or five deans, and in some areas extended to include sub-deans and representatives of the younger clergy) or its Area Senate of Priests. These will meet with the bishop frequently – often monthly. Each deanery has a monthly meeting of all the priests of the deanery, at which the bishop tries to be present. It is now possible for each parish to have confirmations each year, and more frequent visits from the bishop on other parish occasions.

The Cardinal has made the care of his priests one of his principal concerns. He has asked the Area Bishops to give time generously to the priests of their areas. One of his Vicars General is specifically appointed to look after the interests of all the active priests of the diocese; another priest is responsible for seeing to the needs of all the retired clergy.

An innovation of the last ten years (which has required the appointment of a priest as full-time director) has been the adoption of the Ministry to Priests' Programme, for the continuing education of the clergy. The programme is a structured means of ensuring that priests' needs (personal, professional, emotional and spiritual) are catered for. An important lesson learnt from this programme has been the need that a priest has of other priests, and often of a support group, if his personality is to develop healthily. While there is no place for the influence of lay people upon the priest in this programme, a natural corollary of the programme is to help the priest accept that he needs the same kind of support from those he is at pains to serve.

This programme is an official vehicle of priestly growth in the diocese. While priests are free to choose not to participate in the programme, they are required by the Cardinal to account to him for the steps they have taken to ensure their further education. The Cardinal himself participates in the Ministry to Priests' Programme.

In addition to ensuring the care of priests by the establishment of Area Bishops, Vicar General, and Ministry to Priests' Programme, the Cardinal has his own network of personal contacts with his priests. Every priest has his private telephone number and is assured of immediate access without having to use an intermediary. On many occasions he calls together groups of priests (usually by years of ordination) to spend an evening at Archbishop's House – having a meal together and a few hours of companionship. The priests of the diocese know the Cardinal and Area Bishops better than the priests of thirty years ago. With the disappearance of the barriers of those days, an easiness has come about between the Cardinal, bishops and priests that makes freedom and honesty of speech the norm.

The delegation of pastoral care to the Area Bishops has in no way diminished in the Cardinal the concern that every Diocesan Bishop has for sick priests or for those in any way troubled. However heavy his programme may be, he is often the first to visit a sick priest in hospital. It speaks volumes about personal relationships when (as Area Bishops have noted) the first person a troubled priest will turn to is often the Cardinal himself.

The Cardinal, like every bishop, is at heart a priest of the parish, working with and serving people he knows and to whom he is attached. It is his personal touch with those who need his priestly ministry and the effect they will have upon him (out of the distracting range of the television cameras and press reporters) that keep him alive in his vocation.

One of the areas of the Cardinal's pastoral work that will be little known is his meeting at frequent intervals with groups of young people (sometimes a hundred of them together) at Archbishop's House. This is a time for listening to what young people are saying, sharing their anxieties, and supporting them in their faith. Although the meeting occasionally (because of numbers) takes place in the Throne Room, it falls somewhat short of the elegance and formality of the Low Week Meeting. Cardinal Manning, looking down from the oil painting that depicts one of the earliest Low Week Meetings in full fig, must wonder what has come over the Church!

Most of what the public sees of the Cardinal's individual pastoral work is the tip of an occasional passing iceberg. His visits to the Caribbean Festival in Bayswater each year are a good example. Those visits are the least important vestige of a much deeper concern for race relations and the care of the immigrant that have led him not just to set up working parties to advise on problems, but to spend days in East London parishes seeing some of the problems of immigrant lives there for himself.

The area divisions are no barrier to the Cardinal's own prime care for his diocese. He sets his sights on visiting every parish once in three years, usually for one of the big occasions which are family celebrations for the whole community. He will spend the evening with the people, in what the technical jargon will call 'dialogue', but what in fact is a happy and lighthearted time together that is charged with affection. Such meetings are growing-up points both for the Cardinal and for the people of the parish.

The Cardinal's work extends far beyond the Diocese of Westminster. As President of the National Conference of Bishops he will take to heart more than any other bishop in the country the reminder of the Decree on Episcopal Office that 'his task of upholding Christian doctrine is not limited to preaching and catechetical instruction but extends to public statements which, on certain occasions, have to be made and firmly upheld.' This covers a vast area of pastoral care, where sometimes he will speak for the bishops of the country but often will have to speak for himself as the recognized leader of English Catholics. It is in this part of his work that he needs the support of the bishops closest to him, and of lay men and women with the particular expertise and skills that the subject calls for.

The first point made by the Decree on the Pastoral Office of Bishops is that a bishop, while entrusted with a particular diocese, shares a community of care with every other bishop in the world and therefore should show concern for all the churches.

The time spent by the Cardinal with the European bishops, with the Synods in Rome, with the various Roman committees of which he has been the President, might be regarded by some as an invasion upon the time which would be better spent in his own diocese – especially when these Synods and meetings seem to produce such little evidence of the pastoral concern expressed in the preparation for these meetings.

It should not be overlooked that the Cardinal has a role to play here which, flowing from the position of trust which he holds, is as pastorally important as anything he does in his diocese. The cardinals and bishops of the Curial Offices in the Vatican will be dependent upon men like him to distil for them what is happening in the churches – the way the Holy Spirit in the rank and file of the Church is reacting to 'the new order of things in our time'. Should they fail to listen to that message then as advisors to the Holy Father they will fail dismally in their duties, and it will be the Church that suffers. So that perhaps the greatest pastoral service to the Church that men of the stature of Cardinal Hume have to be ready to make, should the occasion arise, is to do for the Pope what St Paul once had to do for his predecessor Peter – save him from the pressure of good men whose eyes and hearts were so firmly fixed on a rich past that they were blind to the richer future ahead of them. That, like so many of the statements, 'which on certain occasions have to be made, and firmly upheld', can make a man like the Cardinal pass through a crucible of misgiving and anxiety; but it will be his own ultimate service of support for, and solidarity with, another successor to the Apostles in the service of Christ.

5

The European Dimension

For Europe the end of the Second World War marked the end of many centuries of pre-eminence in the world. After six years' brutal conflict, large-scale devastation and millions of casualties, both civilian as well as military, the continent of Europe found itself split into two halves separated by a rigid boundary which, thanks to Winston Churchill's 1946 Fulton speech, came to be known as The Iron Curtain.

The historic lands of eastern and central Europe fell under communist rule imposed by the Soviet Union in the wake of its victory over Hitler's armies in the east in 1944–45. For the peoples living in Europe's eastern half, the word 'liberation' had an ironic ring. One tyranny, that of the Nazis, had been replaced by another, that of the Communists. Eastern Europe's new rulers singled out the Catholic Church for systematic persecution. The Catholic press was suppressed; Catholic organizations were banned; and seminaries, church schools and hospitals were closed down. In Czechoslovakia and Hungary most religious Orders were forcibly dissolved. The Eastern Rite Catholic Church, in communion with Rome but with its own Byzantine rite, was officially suppressed in Rumania, and in western Ukraine after it was annexed by the Soviet Union from Poland in 1944–45.

At the height of the post-1945 persecution, four archbishops were deprived of their liberty: Archbishop Josef Beran of Prague, Archbishop Jozsef Mindszenty of Budapest, Archbishop Alojzije Stepinac of Zagreb and Archbishop Stefan Wyszynski of Warsaw. All four became cardinals, but only Cardinal Wyszynski, who was interned from 1953 to 1956, was allowed to resume his episcopal duties. Cardinal Beran died in exile in Rome in 1969, after being forbidden by the Czechoslovak authorities to return home from the consistory in 1964. Cardinal Mindszenty died in exile in the West in 1975. He had spent the period 1949–55 in prison and then, after a brief spell of freedom during the Hungarian revolution of 1956, he sought asylum in the American Embassy in Budapest – and stayed fifteen years. Cardinal Stepinac died in internment in a country parish of his native Croatia in 1960, having spent five years (1946–51) in prison.

Many thousands of priests and nuns were imprisoned throughout eastern Europe during the immediate post-war Stalinist era. So were many lay people, who in addition suffered discrimination at their places of work.

Unlike communist-ruled eastern Europe, western Europe experienced a real liberation in 1945. Full political and religious freedom was restored in countries that had been occupied by Nazi Germany and Fascist Italy, as well as in those two countries themselves. During the first three post-war decades western Europe saw unprecedented economic growth and material prosperity. Fears of further Soviet expansion westward led, in the late 1940s, to the formation of the North Atlantic Treaty Organization (NATO), a defensive military alliance led by the other world super-power, the United States of America. The late 1950s witnessed the emergence in western Europe of a powerful economic grouping, the European Economic Community (EEC), to which most of the non-communist countries of western and southern Europe now belong.

Inevitably, the two halves of Europe drifted apart. Most east Europeans yearn to travel to the West, but are not allowed to, such travel being a privilege granted to only a few. West Europeans can travel to the East but few manage, or bother, to get close to the people living there. Understandably, years of separation have led many west Europeans to look inward. Rather tellingly, when a west European politician, government official or academic talks or writes of Europe, European problems, the need for a stronger Europe or more European unity, what he or she means is not the whole continent, but *western* Europe. This inward-looking west European attitude has, again understandably, become more pronounced in the 1970s and 1980s with the appearance of new, serious problems such as inflation, unemployment and urban violence. And when west Europeans look outwards, it is not usually to the depressing and dismal eastern half of their own continent. Some look to the United States, others to the vast areas of the Third World where west European countries used to have their colonies.

In the spiritual sphere, the growing rift between the two parts of Europe manifests itself in the West in the form of diminishing solidarity with fellow Catholics in the East, while many in the East feel let down and neglected after many years of suffering, even martyrdom. This was not so at the start. In the early post-war years there was strong, unquestioning support among the Catholics in the West for their brethren in the East suffering under Communism. The 'free' felt a deep commitment to help the 'unfree'. But after Stalin's death in 1953 the view gained ground generally in the West – and was reflected among Catholics too – that Communism was beginning to evolve in a more liberal direction, with the prospect of more freedom for all (including of course the Catholics and other religious believers). There grew in the West a feeling that since the communist regimes seemed to be beginning to behave more tolerantly towards their subjects – even to those they had previously persecuted – it behoved those subjects to give their rulers the benefit of the doubt, accept their rule as a fact, and try to come to terms with it in order to carve out a place for themselves in the new 'socialist' order. The unspoken implication was that the east European Catholics should now show more flexibility and prudence rather than heroism and martyrdom. The *Ostpolitik* of Pope John XXIII and, even more, that of Pope Paul VI, reflected this western optimism about the evolution of Communism, but also a certain pessimism about the future of the 'Church of Silence' in the East. This pessimism led the Vatican to negotiate with communist governments in a 'minimalist' spirit of saving what could be saved, particularly the continuity of the church hierarchy. Negotiating with communist governments seemed to those engaged in them on the church side to imply the need to be extremely tactful, not just by playing down the Church's previous strong anti-communism, but also by not airing in public the grievances of the faithful in the East.

For many east European Catholics, this western optimism, apparently shared by secular leaders and churchmen alike, was puzzling, even disconcerting. Like the rest of the population in eastern Europe, religious believers were glad that the era of terror was over. But while grateful for the post-Stalin 'de-terrorization', they could not see any signs of a liberalization around them. The sight of western intellectuals, including priests, 'dialoguing' with east European Marxists who owed their posts to their regimes' favour, was also disconcerting for the local Catholics who had no chance of such a dialogue.

There was another cause of misunderstanding and estrangement. Relying as they did on a strong, self-confident Church as the main bastion in their defence against spiritual strangulation, east European Catholics were dismayed to see many of their fellow religionists in the West apparently hell-bent on dismantling that same Church – allegedly in the name of the Second Vatican Council. This helped to breed among some in eastern Europe a certain mistrust towards the Council itself. Since few from eastern Europe could travel to the West and stay there for any length of time, there was little opportunity for them to appreciate the Council's positive side and the generous impulses that lay behind most of the renewal in the West. This in turn bred a feeling in the West, particularly among the more 'progressive' Catholics, that their east European brethren were reactionary stick-in-the-muds, hopelessly right-wing and all the more likely to be swept aside by history. East European regimes sought to foster this western view by using their own approved spokesmen, some of them inside the churches but operating under the control and direction of the regimes.

More than four decades later, Europe is still divided. The two power blocs still face each other, each under the leadership of a super-power. East-West barriers have not come down, despite more than a decade of negotiations which culminated in the adoption of the so-called Final Act at the Conference on Security and Co-operation in Europe (CSCE) in Helsinki in 1975. The record of the subsequent years, which have seen a number of follow-up East-West conferences in Belgrade, Madrid, Stockholm, Ottawa and in Budapest, with more to come, is not encouraging, particularly in the Soviet Union. There there has been a retrogression in the field of human rights since 1975. But in other east European countries the picture is more varied – and not uniformly discouraging. In some countries – Czechoslovakia in particular – there has been a retrogression. But in Poland, while the 1981 high hopes of Solidarity have been disappointed, the Polish people have managed to win for themselves a greater degree of freedom than has ever before been enjoyed in a country of the Soviet bloc. Hungary, by using very different methods, has evolved a society and an economic system that is very different from that in the Soviet Union. Links with the West, particularly economic ones, matter to the regimes as well. The past couple of years have witnessed the astonishing spectacle of even hardline governments – like that of East Germany – risking the displeasure of the Soviet Union in order to maintain those links. As far as the political and economic spheres are concerned, it can be said that the process of estrangement between the two Europes appears to have been arrested, if not yet reversed.

In the religious sphere, two men have made a particular contribution in recent years. One is Cardinal Hume. The other is Pope John Paul II. Their activities on the European scene since the late 1970s have been a significant factor in reviving the spiritual unity of Europe and giving the divided continent a fresh sense of joint purpose in the religious field. Before the appointment of Abbot Basil Hume of Ampleforth as Archbishop of Westminster in 1976, there had been relatively little awareness of Europe among the English Catholic hierarchy. Inevitably, because of their background, most of the English bishops tended to look westwards, to Ireland, the United States and of course beyond to what used to be the British Empire. The arrival in Westminster of a Benedictine monk, with a French mother, and who had studied at a German-speaking university, taught European languages at Ampleforth, and had strong interest in and links with the Orthodox Churches, seemed to portend a change. In one of its first leaders after the new appointment to Westminster, *The Tablet* wrote perceptively:

> The Archbishop recognizes that his prime duty is towards his diocese but he does not see this in isolation: rather as part of the nation, and he sees the nation in turn as part of Europe. He wants to be in touch with his fellow bishops not only here but on the continent, particularly in western Europe, so that the broad lines of doctrine and discipline may develop on an international scale (*The Tablet*, 27th March 1976).

The outstanding spiritual qualities of the new man in

Westminster were quickly recognized, not only in Britain but also in Europe and beyond. In 1979 Cardinal Hume was elected, to nobody's surprise, President of the Council of European Bishops' Conferences (CCEE). He was re-elected for another term in 1983, which expires in September 1986. In his European role the Cardinal has concentrated on three objectives: the organization of the second 'evangelization' of Europe; bringing the two halves of Europe closer together and thus closing the gap that has started to assume dangerous proportions; and, last but not least, making the whole of Europe, especially its better-off western part, more aware of its worldwide responsibilities, notably towards the Third World.

Cardinal Hume's work, which will be discussed in greater detail below, has been in complete harmony with the ideas and intentions of Pope John Paul II. Europe had been very much on the Pope's mind while he was still Archbishop of Cracow in Poland. An article of his, on the subject of the frontiers of Europe, appeared in the Italian journal *Vita e Pensiero* shortly before his election as Pope. In June 1979, less than a year after becoming Pope, he delivered this passionate appeal during his first trip to Poland:

> The Europe which, during its history, has been several times divided, the Europe which, despite its present and long-lasting divisions of regimes, ideologies, and economic and political systems, cannot cease to seek its fundamental unity, must turn to Christianity. Despite the different traditions that exist in the territory of Europe between its eastern part and its western part, there lives in each of them the same Christianity which takes its origins from the same Christ, which accepts the same Word of God, which is linked to the same twelve Apostles. Precisely this lies at the roots of the history of Europe; this forms its spiritual genealogy. Christianity must commit itself anew to the formation

> of the spiritual unity in Europe. Economic and political reasons alone cannot do it. We must go deeper; to ethical reasons (Czestochowa, 5th June 1979).

In the course of the same historic journey, which exerted enormous impact in Poland and beyond, the Pope wondered aloud:

> Is it not Christ's will, is it not what the Holy Spirit disposes, that this Polish Pope, this Slav Pope, should at this precise moment manifest the spiritual unity of Christian Europe? (Gniezno, 3rd June 1979).

In order to emphasize the spiritual unity of eastern and western Europe still more clearly, in December 1980 the Pope proclaimed St Cyril and St Methodius (two brothers from Salonika who had worked as missionaries among the Slavs) co-patrons of Europe together with St Benedict, whom Pope Paul VI had proclaimed patron of Europe in 1964. In July 1985 the Pope published a full encyclical called *Slavorum Apostoli* and dedicated it to St Cyril and St Methodius. The occasion was the eleven hundredth anniversary of the death of St Methodius in 885.

During his visit to Spain in November 1982, the Pope delivered a declaration to Europe in the course of a European Act in the cathedral of Santiago de Compostella, in the presence of King Juan Carlos and five thousand invited guests, who included leaders of the European Economic Community and presidents of episcopal conferences from all over Europe. Echoing the article on the frontiers of Europe before his election, the Pope said that European frontiers coincided with those of the inroads of the Gospel. Today, he said, the soul of Europe remains united because, beyond its common origins, it has similar Christian and human values. And he called on Europe to find itself again and to be itself, to rediscover its origins, to revive its roots.

A year later, in September 1983, in Vienna, speaking to a crowd of some hundred thousand people, including about seventy bishops from East and West, he emphasized Europe's unity in 'the deep Christian roots and the human and cultural values which are sacred to all Europe'. In an obvious reference to the situation in eastern Europe, the Pope commented that 'unlike the Austria of today – sadly, not all of Europe is free of foreign domination and military violence, free from immediate threat from the outside.'

To study more closely those common Christian origins of Europe, a huge conference was held in Rome in November 1981, with the Pope's enthusiastic support. The organizers were – once again emphasizing both parts of Europe – the Pope's old university of Lublin in Poland and the Lateran University in Rome. This conference illustrated in a nutshell the change in priorities under the new pontificate. It would have been simply unthinkable under Pope Paul VI. He had tended to see Europe as, essentially, the West, and looked upon the East as mainly a diplomatic problem. His *Ostpolitik* was designed to secure a little more breathing space for the Catholic Church in eastern Europe through cautious negotiations with the communist rulers, often conducted above the heads of the local Catholic hierarchies.

Pope John Paul II's policy is based on a grand design which strives for a restoration of European unity not only – or even principally – in the political field, but also and above all in the cultural and spiritual fields. Part of his vision is ecumenical because the Orthodox Church is strong in eastern Europe and indeed is the dominant church in several countries (the Soviet Union, Rumania, Bulgaria and – outside the Soviet bloc – in eastern Yugoslavia). This strength of feeling accounted for the Pope's insistence, in November 1979, on visiting Turkey – despite strong objections from the Turkish government – in order to meet the Orthodox Patriarch who resides in Istanbul.

In an important programmatic address delivered to the

Christian Forum in Ghent (Belgium) in November 1981 (and published as a pamphlet by the Catholic Truth Society in 1982), Cardinal Hume offered his own reflections on the Christian contribution to the future of Europe. Christians, he argued, must be in the forefront of the struggles for human rights and religious freedom. They must be vigilant in their defence of the right to life of the unborn and the handicapped. They must face up to the dilemma of nuclear disarmament. They must be prepared to accept a more frugal life if that is necessary to bring about a more just economic order. In all things, they must follow Christ's example and opt for poverty and powerlessness. The Christian cannot stand aloof from the problems of the modern world, even when involvement brings him into conflict with the spirit of the age. He concluded:

> This continent of Europe and its peoples have a most important role still to play in the modern world . . . The Catholic communities of Europe, east and west, must explore ways of putting into practice their collegial responsibility for the evangelization of the continent. In times past, we took the Gospel to other countries; now the mission field is our own continent. We must not perpetuate the religious divisions of the past. Our mission and our ministry is truly Christian and so it must involve Christians of every tradition, Orthodox, Reformed and Catholic together. We must develop practical co-operation with fellow Christians and explore the consequences of our common baptism, our sharing in the mission of Christ as priest, prophet and king.

Cardinal Hume has sought to put these objectives into practice in two important forums: the Council of the Bishops' Conferences of Europe (CCEE) and, behind the scenes, the Synod of Bishops, on whose standing committee he has represented Europe for a number of years.

Bishops have been around for a long time. The bishop is

both head of his diocese and member of the episcopal college. In addition, various forms of collaboration between bishops have been established at regional level. There have been patriarchates and metropolitan groupings and, during the last century, episcopal conferences in European countries. Episcopal conferences exerted a strong influence during the Second Vatican Council and, after the Council, within the universal Church. Continental bodies are more recent. The Council of Latin American Bishops (CELAM) was set up in 1955. Its European equivalent, the CCEE, was created later – in 1971 – and received canonical approval by Pope Paul VI in 1977. The Council has no power to take decisions binding on individual bishops or their conferences. It exists to foster the exchange of information and to encourage co-operation. CCEE has twenty-five members who represent their countries. The presidium, or standing committee, has three members: Cardinal Hume (President); Archbishop Alojzij Sustar of Ljubljana in Slovenia (Yugoslavia), who is Vice-President; and Archbishop Ramon Torrella of Tarragona in Spain. Delegates are nominated for the following areas: questions concerning the clergy; questions concerning religious orders and congregations; and questions concerning the laity. The Council's secretariat is in St Gallen in Switzerland.

The Council convenes an annual meeting of the secretaries of the different bishops' conferences to exchange information and experiences. From time to time the bishops responsible for particular areas of concern, together with their expert advisors, are invited to meetings at European level, usually in collaboration with the appropriate Vatican department, such as the Secretariat for Christian Unity, the Councils of Laity, Justice and Peace, and Social Communication. CCEE maintains contacts at European level with various church organizations such as the Laity Forum, the Congress of Priests' Councils, the Conference of Religious, Caritas and so on. On the ecumenical front, CCEE maintains close liaison and co-operation with the Conference of European Churches (CEC or KEK) which is the regional organization, with 115 member churches in twenty-six countries, for the non-Roman Catholic churches in Europe. An example of this collaboration was the Ecumenical Encounter, held under Cardinal Hume's presidency, in Riva del Garda in Italy, in October 1984. Some one hundred people, clergy and laity, from the Orthodox, Roman Catholic, Anglican and Protestant traditions studied the implications of a document reflecting on each element of the Nicene-Constantinopolitan Creed of the year 381, under the title 'Our Creed – Source of Hope?' Two previous joint encounters had been held in 1978 and 1981.

Perhaps the most important activity of CCEE is the symposia of European Catholic bishops now organized at intervals of roughly every three years. Usually about eighty bishops attend, with their expert advisors, representatives of priests, laity and so on. Previous symposia (two of them held before the formal setting up of CCEE) have tackled the following themes: diocesan structures after the Second Vatican Council (1967), the life and ministry of priests (1969), the role of bishops in the service of the Faith (1975), youth and faith (1979), the collegial responsibility of the bishops and episcopal conferences in the evangelization of the European continent (1982) and – the bishops' second stab at the evangelization theme – the evangelization of secular society (October 1985).

The most recent symposium attracted the largest attendance so far (120), partly because of the theme but also because of the proximity of the special synod of bishops called by the Pope for the end of November. This was to discuss the implementation and results of the Second Vatican Council on the twentieth anniversary of its conclusion in 1965.

Cardinal Hume used his two addresses at the symposium to affirm the values of Vatican II and its fruits. The Council had helped the Church, he said in his opening address, to move from an attitude towards the world of rejection and condemnation to one of openness, discernment and attentiveness to the 'signs of the times'. The Council acknowledged that the Church profits from the world, he said, and the acceptance of this approach is fundamental for the study of the modern world. Against those who see the widespread changes in contemporary practice largely as evidence of 'decay and breakdown', Cardinal Hume pointed also to 'positive signs of growth and new life'. He summed up his own vision of the Church as 'a communion of the spirit, a *koinonia*' meaning 'a community which talks and listens to others; a communion in which each has proper responsibility and can rely on the support of others; a community which suffers alongside others and brings affirmation, healing and care to those in need.'

A few months before, in an address to a major international symposium on the local church, at Bruges (Belgium), the Cardinal had argued in favour of a revitalization of parish life by the development of small groups of laity within the parish, basing their work on the sacraments of baptism and confirmation; baptism which 'enables those who have received it to share in the priestly, prophetic and kingly role of Christ'; and confirmation which 'equips those who have received it to be witnesses in the world of Christ.' These small groups, he suggested, should learn from the monastic communities which arose in western Europe in the Middle Ages and which were in effect the basic communities of their day. Obviously drawing on his own experience as a Benedictine monk and, indeed, former Abbot, the Cardinal pointed to a carefully worked out balance between the authority of the man in charge and the responsibility of the community:

> St Benedict required the abbot to consult with his community either through the calling of all the

> brethren to chapter or through a smaller body, the abbot's council. Subsequent monastic constitutions, based on the spirit and letter of the Rule, have developed this fundamental characteristic of monastic policy. The abbot is required to obtain permission from the chapter for certain important actions, for others he needs to consult only. Thus the community has some share in the making of decisions and that sharing can indeed be, at times, decisive. The power of the abbot is thus limited by this requirement to consult; it is also limited by the constant reminders made by St Benedict that the abbot must remember to whom he must render an account for his stewardship.

The Cardinal then drew attention to the two chapters in the Rule of St Benedict which instruct the abbot on how to carry out his task:

> These chapters are extraordinarily contemporary; indeed leaders in any walk of life would benefit from a study of them. I do not exclude bishops, busy parish priests or lay leaders.

Or the Pope? The Cardinal always goes out of his way to uphold the institution of the papacy and defend its value and relevance, as he did in a much noted letter to *The Times* on 30th October 1985, in which he took issue with the idea that the Catholic Church was 'still too papal'. Yet his recent contributions, notably the Bruges address and both his interventions at the bishops' symposium in Rome in October 1985, can be seen as a critique of the Church. At a time when Rome seemed to be moving towards a measure of re-centralization, even restoration (to use Cardinal Ratzinger's phrase), Cardinal Hume advocated more listening and consultation, very much as a practitioner of Benedictine-style decentralized leadership himself and also a man of keen political sense, which exists side by side with his outstanding qualities of spirituality. Behind the scenes, the Cardinal, as President of CCEE and also the man representing Europe on bodies preparing both the special bishops' synod of November-December 1985 and the postponed synod on the laity in 1987, has been playing the role of a defender of a liberal vision of the Church and a positive assessment of the fruits of the Second Vatican Council. It is obviously too early for an assessment of his effectiveness, but one thing was quite clear even before the special synod of 1985: he was being listened to with attention, not least by the Pope himself. And if the Catholic Church ends up with a rather more positive assessment of the role of both national episcopal conferences and of the larger, continental episcopal groupings than, for example, that offered by Cardinal Ratzinger in his book *Report on the Faith*, then Cardinal Hume and CCEE under his leadership may be able to claim some credit for this.

On the question of healing the post-war breach in Europe, CCEE has made its contribution in several ways under Cardinal Hume's leadership. For example, his own cathedral in Westminster was the venue for the great Mass, on 27th February 1985, to commemorate the work of St Methodius, on the eleven hundredth anniversary of his death. This Mass, and several other events associated with it in London, not only commemorated the life and work of a great European saint: it was also an occasion to recall the spiritual unity and Christian heritage of Europe, and to pray for the Catholic Church in eastern Europe, deprived for many years of full religious freedom. The unity of the Church in Europe was symbolized by the presence in Westminster of Cardinal Glemp, the Polish Primate; Archbishop Sustar from Yugoslavia; Cardinal Franz König from Austria; and Cardinal Lustiger from France; as well as a number of other bishops from western Europe. Significantly, the Mass was celebrated in English, Latin and Old Slavonic. In a brilliant sermon Cardinal Hume compared

Cyril and Methodius to Benedict – all three monks, but Benedict essentially a community builder, and the brothers playing the role of innovators, missionaries.

Difficulties standing in the way of proper contact between the church hierarchies in eastern and western Europe were demonstrated when, in July 1985, Cardinal Hume, Cardinal Lustiger and Cardinal König failed to get visas to enable them to attend the St Methodius celebrations in Velehrad in Czechoslovakia, where the saint is believed to be buried. The refusal of the Czechoslovak authorities to let them in caused bitter disappointment among Czechoslovakia's Catholics, and unfavourable publicity for the regime in the West. In the end, the authorities relented and allowed Cardinal Casaroli, the Pope's Secretary of State, who had been the Vatican's negotiator with Czechoslovakia in the 1960s and 1970s, to attend. A crowd of 150,000 people – the largest religious gathering in Czechoslovakia ever – turned up for the occasion, and booed the Minister of Culture, Milan Hlusak, when he failed to refer to Methodius as 'Saint'.

The Czechoslovak authorities' 'No' to western bishops was balanced by the Yugoslav authorities' permission for a big celebration in Djakovo in Croatia, also in July. That was attended by Cardinal Casaroli, Cardinal Hume, Cardinal König and a host of other churchmen from both eastern and western Europe.

Leadership in bodies such as CCEE is in many ways a matter of symbolic, public gestures, intellectual stimulation and example and, often, exhortation. But there is also a practical side. An instance of this has been the CCEE's involvement in Polish affairs both during the Solidarity era and since. With the backing of Cardinal Hume, as President of CCEE, a scheme was launched in late 1981 to help private Polish agriculture and thus relieve the sufferings of the population, particularly the old, the sick and people with large families. The Polish bishops, in co-operation with the bishops of western Europe as well as of Canada and the United States, put forward a plan to help private agriculture in Poland by increasing agricultural output and the availability of food, at the same time as improving the social and technical infra-structure in rural areas. The money to allow for the purchase of supplies and equipment not available in Poland was to come from church funds in the West (25 per cent); private grants from bodies such as foundations (25 per cent); and the remaining 50 per cent as grants and credits from the governments of the European Community, the United States and Canada. This imaginative scheme was dealt a blow by the introduction of martial law in Poland in December 1981. But, despite setbacks, the plan has not been abandoned. An Agricultural Foundation has been set up which is independent of Polish state authorities and under the patronage of the Polish bishops' conference. The Polish constitution was amended in July 1983, to guarantee the existence of private family farming in order to help alleviate the fears of private farmers about the possible expropriation of their property. In April 1984 the Polish Parliament passed a law which created the legal basis for the operation of foundations such as the one set up by the Church. However, the authorities have not taken the final step of allowing the scheme to proceed, because of fears within the regime that even a pilot scheme could, if successful, prove too much of a propaganda success for the Church. But neither the Polish Church nor the Church in the West has given up.

Prosperous, highly-developed western Europe has of course a responsibility towards the rest of the continent, and notably towards eastern Europe. But there is also the Third World, with urgent needs that cannot await the outcome of years of patient intergovernmental negotiations – as, for example, during a famine. In November 1984 Cardinal Hume paid a visit to famine-stricken Ethiopia. Afterwards, in his capacity as President of CCEE, he wrote to the presidents of the bishops' conferences of EEC countries, urging them to press their governments to persuade the Community to make funds available for the purchase, dispatch and distribution of 30,000 tonnes of grain and 5,000 tonnes of supplementary foods each month throughout 1985. He also wanted them to raise with their governments proposals about 'aid for rehabilitation and long-term development'. He warned the bishops that 'unless there is investment in agriculture, rural infra-structure and water resources geared to self-sufficiency in food, a similar catastrophe will almost certainly recur within a very few years.' The Cardinal also wrote direct to Dr Garret FitzGerald, Ireland's Prime Minister, who was President of the Council of Ministers of the EEC in the second half of 1984, and to Chancellor Kohl of West Germany and to President Mitterrand of France. His intervention played an important part in securing Community emergency aid of 1.2 million tonnes and the promise of further long-term aid. In March 1985 the Cardinal sent a message to the EEC summit meeting in Brussels, calling for a new initiative from the Community in the face of the continuing famine in Africa.

When Cardinal Hume steps down from the presidency of CCEE later this year (September 1986), he will leave behind him a body of bishops much more conscious of the common problems facing their still divided continent, and of how to tackle them. He will also leave them better aware of what Europe, even if still divided politically, can do for the rest of the Church and the world, particularly the Third World. He has made an important contribution to the understanding of what the second evangelization of Europe – made necessary by the march of secularization (whatever that all-embracing terms means) – should be about. Last but not least, he leaves behind an example of leadership that he consciously based on St Benedict's job description for an abbot, and which he quoted in his address to the bishops in Europe, in Subiaco, in September 1980:

> Let him study rather to be loved than to be feared. Let him not be turbulent or anxious, overbearing and obstinate, jealous or too suspicious, for otherwise he will be never at rest. Let him be prudent and considerate in all his commands; and whether the work which enjoins concerns God or the world, let him always be discreet and moderate, bearing in mind the discretion of holy Jacob, who said: 'If I cause my flock to be overdriven, they will all perish in one day.' So, imitating these and other examples of discretion, the mother of the virtues, let him so temper all things that the strong may still have something to long after, and the weak may not draw back in alarm.

It is against this standard that Cardinal Hume will himself want to be judged as a European church leader when the proper time for such a judgement comes. That time is not yet, because even after laying down his institutional bureaucratic burdens in CCEE he will continue to play an important and influential role in the Church in Europe and beyond.

6

Work for Ecumenism

Cardinal Hume's dedication to Christian unity was vividly symbolized on the day of his installation when, after the ceremonies in Westminster Cathedral, he went with his brother Benedictine monks to nearby Westminster Abbey to sing the old Latin Vespers. It was the first time it had been sung in the Abbey – England's most prestigious Benedictine house of pre-Reformation times – since the final breach between Rome and Canterbury some four hundred years ago. Anglican Benedictines joined their Roman Catholic brethren in the choir stalls. The vast congregation was a mingling of all the main churches.

That bright March day ten years ago is still vivid in the minds of those who attended its solemnities, and especially those of us whose duty it was to report them. Dom Basil's visit to the Abbey completed the cycle of prayer attending his installation. It emphasized the priority of prayer for a monk – particularly a Benedictine – the emphasis of spirituality that has distinguished his time at Westminster, the spirituality that was the fount of the qualities for which he was chosen and which has set him so much apart from his predecessors. It re-emphasized the conviction that still fully inspires his thinking that Christian unity is best achieved by 'praying churches', that the spiritual prompting, the Godward, must be set over against the practicalities of organic unity, the church politics, the commissions and committees, the nuanced exchanges of leaders and pundits. It is something I shall come back to. It is at the heart of any consideration of Basil Hume and Christian unity.

'We have been at prayer together.' So the new Archbishop began his address, thanking the Dean and Chapter of Westminster for inviting them to the Abbey. And he went on to quote John 17: 21, the familiar 'that they may all be one, as Thou Father art one in me and I in Thee; so that the world may come to believe it is Thou who has sent me.' But Westminster Abbey, then the setting of so powerful an act of unity, is also a potent symbol of disunity, of that sequence of history that was beginning when Henry VIII sent on their way the predecessors of the Benedictine monks now gathered there again under the former Abbot of Ampleforth. Within its walls since the break with Rome, have been crowned monarch after monarch, forbidden by law to be Roman Catholic or married to a Catholic, crowned by a Parliament-dominated Church, one of whose articles describes the sacrifice of the Mass as 'blasphemous fables and dangerous deceits', monarchs presiding over centuries of anti-Catholic prescription and persecution whipped up sometimes into anti-Popery mob hysteria, of times of intolerance and disunity and mistrust not only between Catholics and Anglicans and the Free Churches but between them all.

Wounds healed only with time and patience, the new Archbishop told his Abbey congregation. Referring to Roman Catholicism and Anglicanism in particular, he went on: 'Our two Churches give proof of this. Our wounds are ancient; the healing is slow. We have been, I think, like two sisters estranged, not on speaking terms, quarrelsome, misunderstanding each other.' He ended with his summa for unity for his time:

> First we shall not respond to Christ's prayer for unity unless our Churches are praying Churches. We must discuss, we must have commission, we must act together, but none of this will be of any avail unless we pray and pray earnestly. Secondly, we must yield to the claims and demands made by

> truth. Ours must not be the weak, helpless, indeed almost cynical response of Pontius Pilate, 'What is truth?', but it must be a courageous, relentless and honest search for what is the truth about God and His purposes for man, ultimately from Him who is 'The Way, The Truth and The Life'.

And then he sounded a note he has reiterated over the years:

> I have spoken in a great church of the Anglican Communion, but the Catholic Church wishes to speak and to listen to *all men of every religion or of none*, for the good of us all and the greater glory of God whose praises we have been privileged to sing in the Abbey.

It was a heady end to a heady day for that congregation of unity-minded people as the one hundred and fifty black-robed monks filed out of their stalls at the end of the Vespers for the Feast of the Annunciation of the Blessed Virgin Mary. There were thoughts, too, of how earlier on in Westminster Cathedral, almost the first act after his enthronement, he had left the altar to embrace the Archbishop of York and the leaders of other churches. Thoughts of his Anglican father and Roman Catholic mother, that he was the product of a marriage which was in itself an act of Christian unity. Thoughts turned to Dom Basil's time at Ampleforth, of his close friendship with Donald Coggan at nearby York. When the time came for Dr Coggan to go to Canterbury, the Abbot of Ampleforth was in the cathedral for the enthronement at the personal invitation of the new Archbishop. Then, too, there was his active membership of the local council of churches at Ryedale in Yorkshire, his preaching at a number of local Methodist churches. And for four years his chairmanship of the Benedictine Ecumenical Commission. 'Ah,' said a venerable Anglican cleric to me as we left the cathedral, 'with such a man at the head of the Roman Catholic Church here who knows what will happen in the way of unity in the years ahead?' It was the kind of day when you could easily make yourself believe that history could indeed be rolled back a thousand years and the Church undivided.

Ten years on and what now? There has, to my way of thinking, been no peak in the unity experience comparable to the Vespers of Westminster Abbey of 1976, although some, I know, would take issue with me and say the Pope's visit of 1982 was equally significant. Any assessment of Cardinal Hume's work for unity must at this stage of his life and ministry be of an interim nature and in no way definitive. But before attempting even something provisional, it is better to get things in context and look briefly at the overall unity scene. After nearly a century of the modern ecumenical movement there have been only three complete mergers across denominational boundaries. Two have been on the Indian subcontinent where Christians are in a small minority, and the other in this country between English Presbyterians and most of the English Congregationalists who together formed the United Reformed Church, and were later joined by the Churches of Christ.

Unity is often a tormented endeavour, beset by dogmatic rigidity and historic conditioning. Nothing so stirs the contempt of those hostile or indifferent to the religious dimension than the fruitless efforts of the Christian Churches to heal their divisions. But it is usually a contempt born of ignorance or reluctance to comprehend the forces that have shaped organized Christianity since Apostolic times. The Churches are human institutions with the same human fallibilities as any other, resulting in such ruptures as the breach between West and East of the eleventh century and the Reformation itself. It was a Reformation which in this country followed a course unlike that anywhere else, and in so doing has left for Christians today a unique unity situation. But the major issue worldwide is to balance the kind of unity that is desirable with that which is acceptable. Should it be organic unity or some kind of confederation of Churches in inter-communion but with flexible doctrinal and liturgical demands?

Basil Hume is the first Cardinal Archbishop of Westminster completely in the wake of the Second Vatican Council and its decree on ecumenism. How much it has formed his attitudes is readily apparent from so many of his public utterances. His predecessor, Cardinal Heenan, had the unenviable task of mediating the Council to his faithful in its immediate aftermath, as well as of demonstrating to other Churches the thrust of its thinking. He had to face uncouth demonstrations from Protestant extremists as Catholic relations with other Churches quickly gained warmth, not least when he was subjected to constant interruption and abuse from Paisleyites in and around St Paul's Cathedral, when he preached there during a Week of Prayer for Christian Unity. But by Basil Hume's time ardours had been tempered and the only time, so far as I know, that the Cardinal was confronted by Dr Paisley was when he said Mass in the crypt chapel of the Palace of Westminster in July 1978 during the celebrations of the five hundredth anniversary of the birth of St Thomas More.

In Basil Hume there must inevitably be an inbuilt tension over unity. Since adolescence he has been within the ambiance of the Benedictines, the oldest Christian monastic Order, with its constant emphasis on prayer and recollection, but also its stability and its unquestioning loyalty to the papacy. It is an Order that embodies to the full Catholic doctrines, claims, assumptions and attitudes. Not for nothing has it been said of late that perhaps the biggest issue of unity is that of attitudes. Yet if the days have indeed gone when the only Roman attitude to unity was submission, it still follows that there must be give on the Roman side as indeed there must be from the rest. How much give has there been from the Cardinal? How willing is he to take risks? It is not easy.

'Not only should we be praying for re-union but we should be praying ourselves into re-union', the Cardinal has said. 'I would like to see our people coming more and more together to pray.' 'If our people learn to pray together, then they will discover how to engage in joint evangelization effectively', he told the Free Church Federal Council at Newcastle in March 1982, one of his most important unity speeches and one to which I shall return. But apart from the now predictable activities of the Week of Prayer for Christian Unity it is commonly acknowledged that Roman Catholics, Anglicans and Free Church people do not join together for regular prayer for unity on a really widespread scale. There is little enough, too, in the way of joint evangelization and mission.

In January 1983, during the Week of Prayer for Christian Unity, preaching in St Paul's Cathedral without the interruptions his predecessor suffered, he said:

> We have now reached a stage in our journey together when we will have to face honestly and courageously the obstacles which lie ahead. There are many unresolved questions before us all. We need more prayer, study and dialogue on the role of the pope, on the role and mission of the bishops and on the sacraments.

Significantly he added: 'As you well know, it is our Catholic belief that the authority of the Pope has been divinely ordained as the way to preserve truth, charity and unity among Christians.' And in that same homily he said: 'Reconciliation of ministries cannot be cheaply bought, or sought for simple convenience. The progress of reconciling ministries will be long and arduous.'

Perhaps even more revealing of caution was his answer on women clergy to an American questioner in a BBC World Service phone-in. He said:

> I accept the authority of my Church, which does not advocate the ordination of women to the priesthood. The answer given is this is not part of our tradition; and that may be a good argument and that may be a bad argument. I personally, if the authorities of my Church agreed to the ordination of women, would have no problem about it. But I am a man under authority and I would not be in the Catholic Church if I did not accept that.

It was a remark that prompted an American contributor to the letters page of the Catholic quality weekly *The Tablet* to say that one could imagine the churchmen in charge of the Inquisition making the same statement with all possible piety. The writer continued: 'Far better the statement of that Quaker martyr, Mary Dyer, as the ecclesiastical authorities in Massachusetts prepared to incinerate her for "witnessing": "Truth is my authority, not authority my truth." Nowhere in the gospels is obedience singled out as the most necessary virtue, least of all by the Lord, who disobeyed the ecclesiastical authorities again and again when He saw they were patently sinning against the light and the truth.' Succinctly this American writer posed the major unity issue of authority over against conscience, almost as insistent now as it was at the Reformation.

Yet if his public utterances sometimes display the traditional conditioning of his Church and Order, others show how much he is in tune, too, with quite different approaches. It is this process of balancing the conservative with the reformer, the cautious with the adventurous, which makes him one of the most interesting churchmen of his time, although it has to be said again that it is too early to assess the true balance. His instinctive sadness at division is always apparent. He wrote in 1980:

> Christians who are divided from each other are in a poor position to preach peace and reconciliation to an unimpressed world. Religious divisions are a

> scandal. But there are no short cuts to that organic unity which is the aim of all ecumenical endeavour.

And in that speech already quoted to the Free Church Federal Council he said:

> We should not allow the process of working to achieve full organic unity to obscure the fact that there exists already a profound unity among the baptized.

Quoting Vatican II's Declaration on Ecumenism he said: 'We are brothers in the Lord.'

This has to be set alongside an address earlier on, at Chantilly in France, when he said that baptism should lead to a complete profession of faith, for unity in faith was necessary for church unity. 'How will the world believe if among those who teach there is too much diversity and too many hesitations?' he added. But then, almost in the next breath, he was reflecting on Vatican II's thinking on the hierarchies of truth, broadly those things which are indispensable and unalterable and those over which there could be some measure of give and take. 'What sort of pluralism in doctrine is compatible with the one revealed truth?' he asked. 'There can be pluralism of doctrine; there cannot be pluralism in faith.' But then he went on: 'If division is to be healed must we not become much more familiar with one another's doctrinal emphases, our various existential hierarchies of truth?' Later, considering the goal of an undivided Church, he said: 'The question is not what kind of diversity is acceptable but what sort of pluralism is desirable.'

There was, however, one exercise in Christian unity that Basil Hume inherited with the job. It was the deliberations of the Anglican-Roman Catholic International Commission, popularly known as ARCIC and set up jointly by Pope Paul VI and Archbishop Michael Ramsey in Rome in 1968, to study eucharist, ministry and authority. The undertaking tackled by eighteen academics from the two Churches, all of them from the West, was both adventurous and tantalizing. The Reformation in England was a half-cock process which left a national Church see-sawing down the centuries between Catholic and Protestant concepts, a Church claiming to be the continuing Church in England as well as the Church of England and retaining the traditional orders of ministry. The centuries of discrimination against the tiny minority of Roman Catholics, together with a kind of innate anti-Popery, left marked antipathies which the restoration of the hierarchy and Catholic emancipation during the last century failed to eliminate. Until the Second Vatican Council Roman Catholic and Anglican clergy in general were barely on speaking terms, yet a sizeable section of the Church of England was strongly Catholic-orientated in liturgy, doctrine and dogma, intensely so since the Oxford Movement of the 1830s under the influence of, among others, John Henry Newman, the Anglican poet and theologian who became a cardinal of Rome. Yet, as is so often the way among those who have much in common, the things that keep the two Churches apart matter deeply to many of their members. This is something Cardinal Hume understands well from his close friendship with Anglicans. As far back as October 1977 we have him saying that if dialogue between the two Churches was to make progress it must become tougher and more direct. 'We Roman Catholics must make our position absolutely clear. And I think the Anglican Church has to make up its mind what it really believes because the spectrum is too wide.' The irony was that the Anglican Church has spent the last four hundred years trying to make up its mind.

Cardinal Hume's old friend Donald Coggan, former Archbishop of Canterbury and now Lord Coggan, is a strong advocate of inter-communion, something he made perfectly plain in, of all places, Rome itself. But in an address to the General Synod of the Church of England in

February 1978, when he received a rapturous welcome, the Cardinal said bluntly that issues concerning the Eucharist and those connected with the ordained ministry will not be finally and satisfactorily resolved until such time as there is agreement on the nature of the Church. Of inter-communion specifically he added: 'We believe that this sharing pre-supposes not only the same belief in the reality of Christ's presence in the sacred species, but also a common faith in general.' For good measure he re-affirmed Catholic opposition to the ordination of women.

Of the ten years or more of the first round of ARCIC deliberations, no more perhaps need be said of the process of discussion than that the Cardinal, with his background and his instinctive theologizing, must have found the joint team very compatible, scholars admirably equipped to re-solve ancient antagonisms over definitions and able to strike delicate theological and philosophical balances. In fact they achieved what some thought unachievable: sub-stantial agreement on Eucharist and ministry; agreement on some aspects of authority and convergence on others.

It was one thing for academics to agree; quite another for the governing body of the Church of England, the General Synod, and for the conference of Roman Catholic Bishops of England and Wales with Cardinal Hume at their head. In the event the Synod overwhelmingly approved the ARCIC findings – although slightly more reserved over authority than Eucharist and ministry – and sent them off for consideration by the Church of England dioceses and deaneries before a final Synod debate in time for the 1988 Lambeth Conference of worldwide Anglican bishops. Each of the twenty-seven Churches of the Anglican Communion has to make up its own mind on ARCIC. Even more remarkable, and on the face of it less predictable, was the warm general approval of the ARCIC documents by the Roman Catholic bishops, and that in spite of a somewhat dusty first reaction from the Vatican's Congregation for the Doctrine of the Faith – the former Holy Office – at whose head is the much discussed Bavarian Cardinal Joseph Ratzinger. Unlike the General Synod, the Conference of Bishops meets behind closed doors, but even so it is safe enough to assume that Cardinal Hume played a major part in shaping a document now regarded as of major significance in the unity movement.

In short the bishops welcomed 'a very rich and dynamic view on the Eucharist' but noted that although some Anglicans practised reservation and adoration of the Blessed Sacrament, others still found devotions of this nature unacceptable. They approved unreservedly of the findings on priesthood and ordination. Over that most difficult of all issues, the papacy, they felt that ARCIC could be seen as giving insufficient weight to the role of a universal primate, but in the light of history it was not so easy to come to substantial agreement. But the need for continuity of ministry and therefore episcopal authority was clearly stated in a way holding real promise for the future.

The biggest surprise of all was over papal infallibility, perhaps the major stumbling block to unity for most Anglicans. The bishops agreed that the only grounds for complete assurance that an infallible definition had been made was the way it was received in the Church – that Reformation concept of reception acceptable not only to Anglicans but perhaps even more so the Free Churches. On the face of it it would seem that receptionism cuts across traditional concepts of papal authority, certainly across the First Vatican Council doctrine that infallible definitions are infallible of themselves and not because they are afterwards accepted by the Church. That receptionism should have been endorsed by a conference of bishops with a Benedictine monk at their head can be seen as impatience with over-rigid manifestations of traditional papal and curial authority, of the kind thought by some to be personified by Cardinal Ratzinger and his Congregation, so quick to pick holes in the ARCIC findings. It also goes to show how much the Cardinal and his brother bishops value a measure of autonomy for local churches, something so vigorously underlined in their submission for the recent special synod of bishops in Rome to consider the effects of the Second Vatican Council.

Meanwhile the ARCIC documents have gone to Roman Catholic Bishops' conferences the world over, where their reception is being strongly influenced by the favourable reaction of their brother bishops in England and Wales, in the heartland of Anglicanism. Reactions are being collated by the Secretariat for Christian Unity at the Vatican. Presumably the last word – expected in 1988 – will be with the Pope. But on whose advice? Such is the regard for the 'English' Cardinal (he is half-Scottish and half-French) in Rome itself and among the world's bishops, particularly in Europe, that this might be one of the rare occasions in history when the Holy Office, if indeed it felt so moved, might feel itself unable to reverse the recommendations of national churches over the ARCIC documents.

Another of the big stumbling blocks to unity is *Apostolicae Curae*, the declaration by Pope Leo XIII in 1896 that Anglican Orders were invalid, in other words that the Archbishop of Canterbury and his clergy are no more than laymen. In a long interview with me for the *Church Times* on the eve of the 1978 Lambeth Conference, the Cardinal said that *Apostolicae Curae* needed careful reconsideration. In their reactions to ARCIC the bishops took this a stage further, asking whether a public act of convalidation or reconciliation could resolve the situation. Another round of discussions of the issue is believed to be in progress.

Meanwhile a second ARCIC team, set up jointly by the Pope and the Archbishop of Canterbury, Dr Robert Runcie, during their meeting at Canterbury, has already moved towards agreement on another difficult Reformation issue – justification by faith alone. Indeed it seems that all that is now needed is some dotting of i's and crossing of t's. This is something of particular importance for Anglican Evangelicals, but for many other Anglicans it is of lesser significance. The new ARCIC team has also started a serious discussion on the ordination of women, something already practised by some Churches of the Anglican Communion. The Church of England, with threats of split from within, has still to make up its mind. This indeed, is *the* issue on which hopes of unity could founder. But that apart, if the 1982 ARCIC agreements are endorsed by the Lambeth Conference of 1988 and approved by Rome, there seems little reason, in the thinking of some observers, why moves towards the reconciliation of the ministries of the two Churches should not begin. Other observers, certainly, are less optimistic. What is generally agreed is that since Cardinal Hume's appointment new bishops have been created, of different style and attitude to many of their predecessors, men of intellectual openness yet without undue triumphalism but at the same time fully dedicated to the teaching and order of their Church. The Archbishop of Westminster, of course, does not appoint bishops, but his preferences are bound to have been taken into consideration by the Pro-Nuncio in his recommendations to Rome, particularly someone so well attuned to local nuances as the former holder of that office, Archbishop Bruno Heim. The influence of Cardinal Hume on Roman Catholic-Anglican unity is, as with so much that he does, neither flamboyant, nor headline-seeking and sometimes not immediately obvious but quietly, gently and effectively exercised in bishops' conferences and other gatherings and in personal encounters.

The Pope's visit to this country has been rightly seen as an important exercise in Christian unity. But such visits, even with so strong-minded a pontiff as John Paul II, are not undertaken without consultations with local churches, and above all with their leaders. Much of the Pope's visit, especially at Canterbury Cathedral, the mother church of the Anglican Communion, with the historic picture of the Pope and Archbishop at prayer, was very much an exercise in Roman Catholic-Anglican relations. But of the utmost significance in any assessment of Cardinal Hume's attitude was the presence there of leaders of other Churches, and the exchange of the peace between the Pope and themselves, followed by a meeting after the service and the Pope's invitation to them for further talks in Rome. That it was not a predominantly Anglican occasion is thought by many senior Free Churchmen to be largely due to the Cardinal's influence, although it is difficult to imagine Dr Runcie not welcoming leaders of other Churches on such an occasion. There is a strong feeling abroad that however close the Cardinal may feel to Anglicanism through friendship and the many similarities in ministry, liturgy and style between the two churches, his attitudes have nevertheless been consciously shaped to the importance of the Churches of the Reformation in the over-all healing of Christian divisions. (To what extent this is shared by all his brother bishops is something else.)

One of the most interesting aspects of this was how he went out of his way, apparently unprompted, to reassure leaders of the Free Churches in his already-quoted 1982 speech to the Federal Council, that there was no secret deal over unity between Rome and Canterbury as part of the re-establishment of diplomatic relations between the Holy See and Britain. Archbishop Bruno Heim, like his predecessors, was, until recently, an Apostolic Delegate, in other words the Vatican's representative to the local hierarchy but without official diplomatic status. Just before his retirement the Archbishop was upgraded to Pro-Nuncio, giving him ambassadorial rank, with full diplomatic relations between the Court of St James and the Holy See. Our man at the Vatican was similarly upgraded. The Cardinal told his Free Church audience:

> It is, most emphatically, irrelevant to our ecumenical tasks, although it could not have been contemplated without that general lowering of suspicion and fear brought about by the ecumenical movement.

The Cardinal also assured the Free Churchmen that the move was not a preliminary step to constitutional change. With considerable subtlety he left it at that. The Queen, of course, is the supreme governor of the Church of England. Under the Act of Settlement neither the monarch nor the consort may be Catholics. Parliament still has considerable say over the Church of England. The Queen (in practice the Prime Minister) has the final say in the appointment of Church of England diocesan bishops, twenty-six of whom have seats in the House of Lords. And the Archbishop of Canterbury crowns the monarch. Sensitivities both to the Church of England's constitutional links and also, perhaps, to more extreme Protestant opinion, were shown by the last-minute cancellation, for reasons not clearly specified, of plans by the Prince and Princess of Wales to attend the Pope's early morning Mass in his private chapel at the Vatican. To what extent was the Cardinal consulted? Be that as it may, varying aspects of the Anglican Church-State link – of 'establishment' – have stirred misgivings when thoughts turn to unity both among Roman Catholics and the Free Churches. The reference to constitutional change by the Cardinal in that context seemed to show diplomacy of a delicacy unexpected these days in a Benedictine monk.

Yet Cardinal Hume's approach to wider groupings of Christians has been on the whole cautious. Although not involved itself the Roman Catholic Church in this country gave broad support to the idea of the Covenant for Unity. This was an exercise involving the Church of England, the Methodist, United Reformed and Moravian Churches, and came into being in the wake of the failure, twice in ten years, of a plan to unite the Church of England and the

Methodists. In his speech to the Free Church Federal Council in March 1982 the Cardinal, after referring to the Covenant as a highly delicate matter, added this:

> Let me say at once that there is no question of our abrogating to ourselves the role of ultimate judge concerning the way God operates through the ministries of the different churches. That is why, I presume, many wish to avoid using words like 'ordination' or 're-ordination' precisely because it might suggest a denial of the fruitfulness of years of ministry. A ministry which has produced evident fruit, both in terms of producing the Word of God, of witness and of service, could only have done so because it was used by God. On the other hand, it is Catholic belief that it is in accordance with God's plan for His Church that its 'ordering' should be based on the threefold ministry, and that entry into that ministry has entailed ordination. This ordering, I realize, will be the accepted practice of the covenanting Churches after the ceremony of reconciliation. But where I am bound to express considerable hesitation concerns the proposed means of effecting the reconciliation. If the Liturgy for the reconciling of ministries is explicitly not considered to be an ordination to the presbyterate, then the question must be asked: 'Does the ceremony of reconciliation achieve its desired purpose?'

Within weeks the General Synod of the Church of England rejected the Covenant scheme, and it was ambiguity over the method of recognition of ministries which stirred most opposition during the debate. As with the Anglican-Methodist unity scheme, it was mainly opposition among the clergy that defeated the Covenant, with the Anglo-Catholic or 'high church' wing worried about what they saw as dilution of the traditional theology of ministry and order, and the effect this would have on unity with Rome. Another sticking point was women clergy. The Church of

England would have had to recognize the women ministers of the other Churches with which it was covenanting. To what extent the Cardinal's words influenced waverers in the Synod, particularly the failure to reach the majority needed in the House of Clergy, is anyone's guess. It is significant that there has been an increase of late in the number of converts from the Church of England to Rome, including a few clergy of distinction. This is thought in some cases to be as much due to the Cardinal's qualities of leadership and priesthood as to discontent with the Church of England, particularly the possibility of ordaining women, and doctrinal controversy.

But most intriguing and not easy to explain simply have been attempts to persuade the Roman Catholic Church to become a full member of the British Council of Churches, particularly since Dr Phillip Morgan became General Secretary in September 1980. But as far back as 1978 Cardinal Hume told me in an interview that the Roman Catholic Church was uneasy about certain positions bodies such as the World and the British Councils of Churches held over matters to do with moral theology and ethics, such as euthanasia and abortion. 'We could not involve ourselves in movements which, although they do an enormous amount of good, could nevertheless compromise our position on such matters', he added. On another occasion the Cardinal told me of his 'hesitations' about the presently-constituted British Council of Churches as an effective instrument for Christian unity.

Yet the Roman Catholic National Pastoral Council of May 1980 in Liverpool, with unity the topic first on its agenda, recommended by a big majority, and to the overwhelming applause of delegates, that:

> Since our remaining outside the British Council of Churches puts a permanent question mark against the serious commitment of our Church in this country to the cause of Christian unity, we strongly

> urge the bishops to reconsider the question of the entry of the Catholic Church in England and Wales to the British Council of Churches.

The response of the bishops was basically cautious and noncommittal.

The attitude of a Roman Catholic leader such as Cardinal Hume to the modern ecumenical movement and its offspring, the World and local Councils of Churches, cannot be assessed without a glance at their background. Early initiatives came mainly from within Western Protestantism. Its mark is still there, although some episcopal churches, including the Anglican and the Eastern Orthodox, are members of the World Council (set up in 1948) and regional and national councils. Since the Second Vatican Council Roman Catholic observers have attended their proceedings. In a few cases local Roman Catholic Churches are full members of national councils. In this country, with official blessing, Roman Catholics are full members of most local councils of churches, and take part in varying degrees in about a sixth of the country's four hundred and fifty or so local ecumenical projects – areas especially dedicated to the processes of unity.

Cardinal Hume is by no means alone in his hesitations about the British Council of Churches. They are heard in the deliberations of the governing bodies of some member churches, particularly the General Synod of the Church of England. They are made clear enough in letters to church newspapers. For a start the Council does not officially initiate or negotiate unity moves between member churches, although it can be a force behind the scenes. There is no central authority, no assembly of church leaders whose decisions would be accepted by all member churches. The decisions of the twice-yearly gatherings are advisory and not mandatory. They are reached by the essentially Protestant process of assembly voting of clergy and laity.

The BCC, like the world body, is noted for massive output of lengthy papers on a variety of international and national issues, sometimes couched in socio-political terms known by the irreverent as 'ecumenese'. It shares with the world body criticism for left-wing leanings. It has been thought by some as more pluralistic than definitive in its approach to ethics and morals. Moreover, regardless of the Lund Principle (named after the Swedish city where it was formulated by a World Council conference in 1952) that Christians should do everything together except what conscience forces them to do apart, the member churches of the BCC have tended to go their own ways on a wide variety of endeavours. An exception is the BCC's highly-effective international aid organization – Christian Aid. Added to all this is the relative indifference of the secular media to the deliberations and activities of the Council.

Moreover, talks with Anglicans are only part of many bilateral conversations between the Roman Catholic Church and other churches and groupings, including Orthodox, Methodists, Lutherans, Pentecostals and the Alliance of Reformed Churches. Although as far as I know Cardinal Hume has not made his own thinking public on this issue, there certainly is within Roman Catholicism the feeling that the Church has made its commitment to unity abundantly clear in these bilateral conversations. What more could be achieved by membership of the BCC as it now is? Yet there is a feeling among some influential members of the Council, and indeed among some of the Roman Catholic bishops, that a British Council of Churches without Roman Catholic membership is an anachronism and could lead to atrophy. Certainly since the Pope's visit there has been a more intense effort than ever before to engage the Roman Catholic Church more fully. Dr Morgan says that the Council, after forty-two years of life, has stated its willingness to change, to become whatever more appropriate ecumenical instrument is required.

He also makes the point that the precise concept of magisterium of the Roman Catholic Church is not held by any other Church.

Now a new three-year initiative is under way with the full support of the Cardinal and his Church. It came in the wake of a number of top-level meetings between Roman Catholic and other churchmen. Then at their assembly in March 1984 the BCC called for a new enterprise including Churches not members of the Council. Thirty-two Churches are taking part in an exercise called 'Not Strangers but Pilgrims' including Roman Catholics, and also some small Churches, among them Black Pentecostals. The focus is the nature of the Church. Nationwide local discussions, mainly house groups with the emphasis on the laity, have been taking place. They have been based on local radio and a resource book prepared by Canon Martin Reardon of the Church of England Board for Mission and Unity. They will be explored and assessed. The Churches taking part will then say how they understand the nature and purpose of their Churches and their part in the mission to the world. Finally, in 1987, there will be a series of regional meetings followed by a national conference.

The Cardinal and other church leaders hope that notions of what the Church is will be clarified, ambiguities over the nature of the Church resolved and that this will lead to a body acceptable to Roman Catholics – a body with authority and able to speak for the vast majority of Christians in this country, making it particularly effective in dealing with government over matters of Christian concern. It is hoped that it will be a more potent force for unity. Whether something like this works out it is impossible to forecast.

If, however, we are to take the Cardinal at his word, and he returns to monastic life at 65, neither the BCC round of talks nor the Anglican-Roman Catholic agreement will then have reached anything like fruition. Full commitment to unity will only be found locally among the ecumenical projects and covenants and the house churches, but always with the possibility of them hiving off through impatience with the unity hesitations of the institutional Churches. The danger of a new wave of sectarianism is always there, even for Roman Catholics.

Cardinal Hume's contribution to unity will, I think, be seen as comprehending but careful, a blending of the desirable with the possible. He has shown himself both realist and catalyst. It may well be that moves between Rome and Canterbury have been more positive in his time than between Rome and the Free Churches, but the reunion contemplated is with an episcopal and eucharist-centred Church, indeed a Church that according to some reckoning of history is more in schism than in separation. Yet he will be seen as someone who has done his utmost to comprehend the theology, doctrine and above all style and traditions of the Free Churches. Some see him as more in sympathy with evangelical doctrinal and scriptural absolutes and the moral and ethical principles that stem from them, than with the more radical elements of contemporary Christianity. But above all he has earned his place in the history of the twentieth-century unity movement by bringing it to the spirituality and prayer life of his Order, its blending of community and authority. Its simple black habit seems so much more right for him than the panoply of prelacy.

That the Churches must be together in the Spirit and in a common faith before they can be together as a body, that praying themselves into unity must come before talking themselves into unity, that without prayer anything else is unlikely to be accomplished, such thoughts indeed may be the fount of the one great Church to come.

7

Ten Years at Westminster

The task of assessing a public man in mid-career is a delicate one. His projects are unfinished; his papers are private; his thoughts are his own. No one knows whether the main features of his life so far will be those by which he is eventually remembered and measured, or whether events may yet put all that has gone so far into the shade. Cardinal Basil Hume, by his personality and by the nature of the job he does, has not emerged in his first ten years as Archbishop of Westminster as the sort of forceful leader who can give every circumstance his own distinctive character. It would not be true of him to say that his leadership has made things happen; more subtly, however, he has certainly by his presence *enabled* things to happen. It is somewhat disconcerting to find that, at the outset of his public career, that is exactly what he said he wanted to achieve. He set out to make space for others; and he succeeded. It was a very considerable success.

It began with 'the Hume phenomenon'. The Catholic Church of England and Wales – the two countries share one hierarchy – had a very definite image and character in the years up to 1976, the year of Hume's sudden appearance on the national scene. It was dominated by the personality of Cardinal John Heenan, who was himself the last of a line of Archbishops of Westminster stretching back to the first, Wiseman, all of whom took for granted certain principles and attitudes, both about their own office and about the Church they led.

It was plain from the start that Hume was neither willing

nor able to fit into the Heenan-Wiseman mould. He emerged as the number one choice of the then Apostolic Delegate, Archbishop Bruno Heim, largely because the Catholic Church seemed to be travelling both too slowly and in the wrong direction. Heim was a willing accomplice in a search, with which various leading Catholic laymen were also associated, for a man who could increase the pace and change the direction. But so firmly was the remainder of the English hierarchy soaked in the earlier tradition, that not one of them stood out as promising something different. Indeed, before Pope John XXIII and the Second Vatican Council, which ended a decade before Heenan's death, it had not seemed possible that there could be changes of direction in a Catholic Church so weighed down with its own history. The Apostolic Delegate himself, however, was a protégé of John XXIII; and he came from outside English Catholicism, without any commitment to share its inherited self-understanding.

It is this English tradition of Catholicism which was brought rather abruptly to a conclusion with the appointment to Westminster of the almost unknown Abbot of Ampleforth, and it is the key to the explanation of the surprise and delight with which the public responded to him. Wiseman and Pope Pius IX had, in 1850, established a new Catholic hierarchy – the word they used, revealingly, was 'restored' – which was founded upon the premise that the claims of the national church, the Church of England, were not only quite false but also very nearly dishonest. It was, they believed and implied by their actions, not really a Church at all but an imposter. If true Christianity was to be preached and practised in England, they would have to set up afresh a new organization to do it.

Under both Wiseman and his even more triumphant successor Cardinal Manning, there was a strong belief that the English people would quickly and almost instinctively be able to tell the true Church from the false one, once they were seen side by side. The project was no less than 'the conversion of England' back to what they held to be its own ancient faith. There was no thought of church unity, no scope for co-operation between the rival Churches. The spiritual ministrations of the Church of England were to be spurned, and the Catholic people protected from contamination by them.

It did of course fail. The English were not swept off their feet; indeed they continued to regard the Roman Catholic Church as an odd and alien institution, difficult to deal with and difficult to trust. The failure of this bold and impertinent scheme, by the church set up by Wiseman and confirmed by Manning, must have been obvious from the outside by the early years of this century, but bodies created to perform certain distinct purposes do inevitably go on trying to perform them, 'going through the motions' long after it becomes apparent that they will not succeed. It may have gone on much longer, but for the extraordinary upheaval in Catholic thinking which came with and from the Second Vatican Council. The Church discovered that changes in direction were not only possible but essential; and 1976, with the appointment of George Basil Hume, marks the year that this truth finally arrived on English shores.

He was an almost instant success precisely because he was so different. From the first, the public warmed to him. It was quickly noted that his style was attractive to that very public which was so unimpressed by the tradition of Catholic leadership of his predecessors. Indeed, the story is told of a television 'vox pop' exercise, not long after his appointment, when half a dozen random passers-by were stopped in the street and asked, on camera, if they could name the Archbishop of Canterbury. The first five could not; the sixth, the proverbial 'little old lady', smiled sweetly and said: 'Why, isn't it that nice Cardinal Hume?' And in the peak years of 'the Hume phenomenon', the late seventies, Anglican clergy could be heard muttering darkly that the spiritual leadership of the nation had crossed the river from Lambeth to Westminster. It was never really so; but it seemed so.

If one supposes that there was a guiding strategy to Cardinal Hume's first ten years – which is not of course the case – the significance of that early period is that it acted for the Catholic Church as a kind of re-launch of an updated product, the necessary preliminary for it to build itself a new relationship with the English nation. The point of a re-launch, as a marketing technique, is that it corrects an image and attracts public attention for the product in its new guise. In this case it just happened that way; there are no marketing experts in the Catholic Church, whose attitude to public relations is quite unsophisticated. But had there been, they could hardly have handled it better. For a while, Cardinal Hume was a hot media property, constantly in demand for interviews, features of the 'day-in-the-life-of' kind in the colour supplements, and for personal appearances.

He was not a man who enjoyed being the object of a personality cult – but that only fed the appetite. On the death of Pope Paul VI, and soon after of Pope John Paul I, Cardinal Hume touched the peak of his personal popularity with wild speculation in some newspapers that he could even be the next Pope. His self-effacing denials – 'I would not have been good at it' – were more grist to the same mill. Who could resist a man who admitted to journalists that he had followed his rating in the papal stakes run by the bookmakers, and had been 'offended' – as he jocularly put it – when the odds started to lengthen?

The significance of his public popularity lay elsewhere. It gave a tonic to the rest of the Catholic Church in England and Wales, which had been at first a little sceptical about the capacity of this outsider to provide the sort of leadership demanded, and it gave confidence to those concerned with the future shape of the Church that this was the right way to go. His appointment was, after all, an experiment by the Apostolic Delegate and by Rome, and they had no way of knowing how it would work. That it did work was the green light they had been looking for, to continue the remodelling of the English Catholic leadership along the same lines. And this is the first, and possibly most important, way in which Cardinal Hume's presence has had a crucial enabling effect. The ten years since his appointment have seen a succession of other appointments to the episcopacy in the Catholic Church in this same 'Hume' mould, so different from that of the previous generations of English Catholic churchmen. Had he failed, the prospects for this transformation of leadership would not have looked good. And there is the stark warning of the Catholic Church in Holland to show just how badly wrong things could have gone.

The end of the first few years of Cardinal Hume's presence at the top brought an event which was to confirm and underline this new sense of direction, the National Pastoral Congress at Liverpool. Delegates from all over England and Wales gathered for a quite unique event in the life of the Catholic Church, uncensored public discussion by a cross-section of the Church's membership, of all that was right and all that was wrong. In its way it was as significant as Hume's appointment itself, but it is very likely that the one would not have been possible without the other. Nevertheless Hume did not play a strong leadership role in the Congress, and at times he even seemed to be slightly out of step with it. The Congress was far more the brainchild of the Archbishop of Liverpool, Mgr Derek Worlock, a man who is in many respects more radical than Hume; but in many subtle ways Worlock needed Hume's support and influence, as indeed was the case in reverse. These two men were by this time dominant influences in the Church, as was shown by their respective positions as President and

Vice-President of the Bishops' Conference. Tacitly at least, each could be said to have a sort of implicit veto over the other, so that for a thing to happen in the Church, the consent of both was necessary. Cardinal Hume perhaps never completely saw the point of the Liverpool Congress, though it is doubtful whether he had any strong objections. It just was not the sort of occasion in which he was entirely comfortable.

It demonstrated for all to see, however, that the Catholic community in England and Wales had already moved a long way and was still in motion. No longer could it be described as supine and unthinking, conservative and self-preoccupied. It demonstrated above all that Hume's appointment in 1976 had come just in time to avoid a dangerous gap opening up between the Catholic episcopal leadership and its lay leadership, as represented by the articulate lay people who attended Liverpool in their hundreds. To the other bishops, also, many of whom pre-dated Hume and were therefore among those who had been passed over in the 1976 appointment, it proved that there had been a fundamental change in the temper of English Catholicism. Some of them even found themselves rather liking it. Hence the Congress in Liverpool in 1980 could well be seen historically as a confirmation and endorsement of the thinking behind the appointment of Hume four years earlier.

Two specific issues emerged from that Congress which were soon after to put to the test the concept of leadership which was represented by the Hume-Worlock axis in the Bishops' Conference. And because of the appointment in 1978 of a new forthright and morally conservative Pope, the political climate was such that their handling of these issues would prove a real challenge. In effect, the Liverpool Congress asked these two, Hume and Worlock, to take a message to the international synod of bishops which was meeting later that year, asking the Church to alter its policy on two extremely difficult and sensitive matters: contraception and divorce.

To Archbishop Worlock fell the task of arguing the case for some easement of church discipline towards Catholics who remarried after divorce, and who, under traditional custom, were deemed to be living in such open violation of the Church's teaching on the indissolubility of marriage that it was not appropriate for them to receive Holy Communion. Lay opinion expressed at the Congress was that this was too harsh. To Cardinal Hume fell the even more tricky question of birth control: the Congress asked that the case should be put for some 'development' of the Church's traditional position, some rethinking, in other words, of the absolutism of the 1968 encyclical *Humanae Vitae*. The international synod in Rome later that year was to discuss 'the family', and hence was bound to discuss these two problems.

The climate in Rome was not favourable. Pope John Paul II had been preaching weekly homilies on the subject of the family which left no one in any doubt that he was in no mood to compromise. The synod was clearly being quietly pressurized, in this and other ways, towards re-endorsement of the traditional positions on both items. Hume, who in Liverpool sat quietly at the back of the discussions on contraception, now had to stand forward and speak against the manufactured tide of opinion in Rome, to put the case for 'development'. And he did so brilliantly. In his synod address, he put his finger on the key theological point in *Humanae Vitae*, the phrase 'intrinsic evil' with which Pope Paul, in the encyclical, had categorized the use of contraceptives in intercourse. Hume asked, innocently enough, what it meant, exactly. There was no more telling way of putting his case. This phrase lay at the very heart of the encyclical's argument. It is the sort of expression that everyone assumes everyone else understands, if they do not themselves. It had passed into Catholic thinking in the simple and understandable form of the principle that the use of contraceptives was always seriously sinful. That may be what it implies: it is not what the phrase means, in itself.

It was the sort of point which could be raised without challenging *Humanae Vitae* directly, yet to answer it would require the whole issue of contraception to be re-opened at the most profound level of moral analysis. And if it did not mean what everyone had assumed it to mean, in their attempts to make sense of it in everyday life, then the door was opened to the possibility of the sort of development of teaching away from the absolute blanket-ban on contraception which had been assumed to be the unyielding Catholic position.

Hume spoke well, also, about the dilemma of ordinary Catholics, faced with what they assumed to be this constant tradition, saying many of them were conscientious and faithful members of the Church. In another address, he spoke of his vision that *Humanae Vitae* was indeed a prophet voice in the world today, thus making it clear that a way forward could perhaps be found which would not require *Humanae Vitae* to be repudiated. That, of course, was the stumbling block for any Catholic who wanted some change in the Church's position on contraception: it seemed to imply what Rome could hardly admit to, that the tradition had got it wrong. So to praise *Humanae Vitae* was a shrewd move: it gave the Pope an opportunity, had he wanted one, to open the question again without putting at risk papal authority. He was looking for no such avenue, as he made clear in his closing address.

Archbishop Worlock fared no better in his separate plea for some amelioration of the position of divorced and remarried Catholics. The Pope firmly slammed the door – and two Englishmen had to return to Britain empty-handed. There was a good deal of despondency in the party that came back. But it seemed to have taught the Cardinal a valuable lesson. It was not enough to be right. To gain your point in Rome, you had also to be political.

The immediate sequel to the Congress in 1980 was the visit of Pope John Paul II to Britain in 1982. The invitation went out from the English bishops at a time when it was thought very questionable whether the Pope could visit Britain at all, because of the long and painful history of relations between the British State and the Holy See. But from a churchman's point of view, there was an even greater danger. It was that the Polish Pope would so misread both the climate of British public opinion and the state of Catholicism in Britain that his contributions during his visit would be counter-productive. It was clear already that he had no great sympathy for the secularized West, which seemed to him to have gone spiritually soft. With his new-found wisdom, knowing that if the visit was to be a success a good deal of 'political' preparation would be necessary, Cardinal Hume embarked on a long and detailed process of briefing the Vatican and the Pope, to leave as little as possible to chance and therefore to eliminate as far as possible the risk of accidental blunders.

The briefing was conducted with such care that when he eventually came, the Pope never put a foot wrong. It was the one totally successful visit of his reign, a triumph both for him and for those who had advised him. It was Hume's triumph too. Somehow the English had succeeded in gaining the Pope's trust, so that he accepted the advice he received, even to the extent of soft-pedalling on contraception. And it may well be that a crucial element in establishing that trust was the Pope's intuitive recognition of Cardinal Hume as a genuinely and profoundly spiritual man, not a Westerner who had gone soft (like so many he could no doubt have named).

The story of that visit is also of course the story of the Pope and the Falklands crisis; of his dramatic invitation to both British and Argentinian church leaders to join him at a Mass for peace in Rome at the height of the conflict, and of his agonized search for the right thing to do in an unprecedented situation. That he was persuaded that a Pope might visit a country at war was again a mark of his trust and esteem for Hume. We do not know the arguments in detail. We do at least know that the English Cardinal pressed the Pope not to do anything which would have scandalized the parents of Argentinian soldiers on the Falklands battlefield. It was a magnanimous point to make; and it enabled the Pope to find a way to make the visit after all. It is said that the turning point in his decision was the personal letter he received from the Archbishop of Canterbury, Dr Robert Runcie. And it is surely inconceivable that Dr Runcie would write such a letter without knowing in advance that Cardinal Hume needed just that kind of support at that crucial moment. To call such tactics 'political' is not to rate them as any less sincere, or to dismiss them as mere manipulations. But the affair showed to Hume, a man distrustful of manipulation in any form, that it was possible to 'play one's cards right' without sacrificing integrity or sincerity.

The papal visit, a success for Hume in the most difficult circumstances conceivable, represented the firm consolidation of his leadership of English Catholicism and his own growth in stature as an international Church statesman. If the first phase of his public career was 'the Hume phenomenon' of the middle and late seventies, and the second the Liverpool Congress and the papal visit, the years since have marked the start of a third phase, possibly the most important of the three.

Gradually, in the years since 1976, the fresh spirit of Catholic leadership originally represented by Basil Hume and Derek Worlock had broadened out to become the common attitude and approach of all the Catholic bishops of England and Wales. On the retirement of the Apostolic Pro-Nuncio, Bruno Heim, in 1985 it was noted that all but one of the diocesan bishops of England and Wales had been appointed during his delegacy, all of them therefore to some extent representing the same sort of policy as that which took Hume to Westminster in 1976. And it has been noticeable, over that decade, how the various policies adopted by the Catholic bishops have gradually become more 'progressive', to use a short-hand term, as the number of 'new' bishops gradually grew, first into a majority and then into a full house. That Rome allowed Archbishop Heim to continue to find men for vacant sees according to this fresh model of what an English Catholic bishop ought to be, is itself an endorsement of Cardinal Hume. It implied continuing trust in English Catholicism. Various attempts to disturb that trust, in the course of the decade, came to very little. Even Cardinal Hume's firm handling of Opus Dei, a right-wing Catholic organization dear to the Pope's heart, did not appear to have counted against him.

In the current phase in English Catholicism, therefore, there is less to be seen of the distinctive leadership of the Hume-Worlock axis, and other bishops have been able to influence developments, perhaps even further and faster than those two senior statesmen would themselves have pressed for. It is a compliment to Hume that he has not dominated the Bishops' Conference, as he undoubtedly could have done, but instead made space for others.

Early in 1985 the bishops issued a remarkable theological document, their considered response to the 'final report' of the (first) Anglican-Roman Catholic International Commission. It was not only remarkable for the warmth of its response, and for its apparent indifference to the views of the Sacred Congregation for the Doctrine of the Faith, which does not like the ARCIC final report. What was striking about it above all was that it made a fresh and fundamentally important contribution to Catholic theology on the vexed question of the infallibility of the Pope. It was not by any means primarily Hume's work, though he endorsed it. It was accepted unanimously by all the bishops, and that was indeed primarily Hume's achievement. Only the president of the bishops could have encouraged and shaped the internal debate to the point where complete agreement emerged, especially with such a sensitive matter as papal infallibility at the centre of the argument.

But even that was to be upstaged later in the year, when the bishops of England and Wales published their submission to the extraordinary synod which the Pope had called for November 1985. For the first time ever, the leaders of English (and Welsh) Catholicism admitted publicly that they found fault with many detailed aspects of the Vatican's administration of the Church, and called for corrective action. In particular, they summoned the Church to be faithful to the Second Vatican Council decree *Lumen Gentium*, the constitution on the church which had presented a new conception of Roman Catholicism.

There is no question that Cardinal Hume has a single-minded commitment to *Lumen Gentium*. It is mentioned more and more often in his speeches. There is not much room for doubt, also, that he has decided, rather against his own inclinations, that *Lumen Gentium* needs some weight behind it if it is not to be lost and forgotten; and that therefore the time has come again for the employment of 'politics' – in the church sense – by the Archbishop of Westminster. It was certainly less than an accident that the English bishops' statement was one of the first to be published anywhere in the world, in the period of preparation before the extraordinary synod. It was less than an accident that it was seen internationally as a rallying point for all those church leaders throughout the world who were becoming anxious about the state of the Church, and who feared that an attempt was about to be made to drag it backwards. It was less than an accident that Cardinal Hume happened at the time to be President of the European Council of Episcopal Conferences, or that he presided over a crucial meeting sponsored by that Council in Rome just before the synod. It was no accident that the key text of his addresses to that meeting was *Lumen Gentium*.

What had happened, in fact, was that Hume began to realize, perhaps long after everyone else did, that he was in a position to make a significant contribution to the health of the whole Catholic Church. He had the English bishops behind him – even, to some extent, ahead of him. He had great reserves of goodwill with the Pope himself. He had his position as President of the European Council of Episcopal Conferences. He had his experience of dealing with the subtleties and intricacies of the Vatican machine. And he had, of course, nothing to lose: the freedom of the man without ambition who did not even want the powerful position he had been given, let alone more power yet.

He is seen, now, by international observers of the internal politics of the Catholic Church, as one of its very key figures. It was absurd to suggest that he might have been made Pope in 1978. It is by no means absurd now to suggest that, should the See of Rome fall sadly vacant in the next five years, he will be one of the front-runners. But whatever the outcome of such a conclave, he will be one of the most influential cardinals present at it, if not Pope then 'pope-maker'. Perhaps he is right, and he would not make a very good Pope. Perhaps indeed, what the Roman Catholic Church will most need, after the glories of the present papacy, is a 'not-very-good-Pope'. Should any cardinal find himself trying to twist the arm of this very English Cardinal, should such an eventuality ever arise, that is probably the only argument that would work with him. For no one will ever persuade George Basil Hume that it is his destiny to be A Great Man.

When he moved into Archbishop's House, Westminster, and before the furniture could be rearranged more to his liking, he worked with the furnishings and dispositions of his predecessor, Cardinal Heenan. On his desk was an old-fashioned telephone with buttons for various extensions, including one marked 'HE'. It was, he said, a continuing mystery to him for weeks, what 'HE' might refer to. Eventually he could contain his curiosity no longer, and asked one of the nuns. It stood for 'His Eminence'. It meant him. It had never crossed his mind.

8

A National Figure

Basil Hume is the most truly national English cardinal of the modern era. In ten years he has become part of the furniture of English life, his place on the stage firmly fixed and universally respected. His standing is recognized as widely among non-Catholics as among the Catholic flock, and his words have their impact on an audience far beyond the confines of the Church. This could not be said with similar confidence of all his predecessors. But when this Cardinal speaks, he is heard as someone more acceptable and decidedly less alien than the voice of Rome. He has inserted himself into the national consciousness. Much as he would detest the idea, one might cautiously place upon him the label of a national institution.

This is partly because times themselves have changed. The Catholic Church remains a minority sect in Britain but is no longer a marginal contributor to the spirit of the age. Such an evolution is not due to one man, or even several men. The process of Catholicism's reception into the full body of national life has been going on for a generation. The informal, and occasionally institutional, impediments to Catholics rising to the top of public life have been steadily whittled away. Important power centres – *The Times*, the BBC, the Cabinet Office – had been colonized by Catholic leaders before Father Basil descended from Yorkshire to London. This opening up of the Establishment probably made it easier for any new leader of the Catholic hierarchy in 1976, a moment of change and renewal, to be himself made welcome.

All the same, the man has made a special mark. The 1980s are the first time it has been plausible to contend that, as a representative spiritual voice, the Archbishop of Westminster counts for as much as the Archbishop of Canterbury. And this is more than somewhat odd. That Basil Hume should have been the vehicle for this shift was a little improbable. No Church leader becomes a national figure without becoming a public performer, speaking to the issues people care about – which encompass many matters that rarely intrude upon the diurnal life of monasteries. It is to his pronouncements on great matters of secular controversy that the public has become accustomed to look in assessing the calibre of an archbishop. Although, as Abbot, Father Basil was scarcely a recluse, he was not appointed to Westminster because of his talents as a public man.

He was particularly inexpert in politics. He had strong views about the Church's lack of clarity at certain moments in the past, but the formulation of positions and the making of speeches on secular matters did not come naturally to him. In the grimier aspects of political life – manoeuvring in the media, lobbying for support – he was a complete innocent. He was a holy man, whose large gift for communication was confined to the spiritual field.

This had to change and, with caution and modesty, it has done. To an extent the Cardinal has fulfilled the norm expected of Church leaders in a secular age. He has made links between the life of the world and the life of the Church in important areas. As they have come over to the public, these can be grouped into four categories, relating to Ireland, to Latin America, to overseas aid and to the great question of nuclear deterrence. This leaves in a separate category his active interventions in debates quite central to the Church's interests, on abortion and genetic engineering, as well as initiatives he has taken as Archbishop of Westminster in such parochially contentious matters as the abolition of the Greater London Council. What is most striking, however, about his major contributions on political matters is how selective they have been. This is a pretty short list. Paradoxically, the Cardinal who has been most warmly welcomed into national life turns out to be the one who has been most sparing in his contributions to it.

Ireland was among the earliest issues the new Archbishop took most seriously. For any Catholic leader, with a substantial Irish flock, it is bound to bulk large. But Basil Hume, looking at it from the monastery, had identified it as one clear case where the Church's own position in the midst of bombing and political impasse appeared to be one of silent paralysis. There was, however, an administrative problem, which has never been properly resolved. The jurisdictional divide between the English and Irish hierarchies, with Ulster falling into the Irish domain, meant that anyone from Westminster had to tread carefully. The Cardinal sought to overcome this at an informal level, setting much store by forming a working relationship with the Primate of All Ireland, Cardinal Tomas O'Fiaich. Few of his initiatives became public events, but he has taken an eloquent stand on some of the awkward ethical questions raised by resistance to British rule – for example, by unambiguously condemning the hunger strike at the Maze Prison in 1980. As a prelate of Franco-Scottish rather than Irish ancestry himself, he could perhaps speak with more clear-headed candour than most about such a grotesque aberration in the cause of Irish republicanism. The Hume approach involves genuine and active compassion for individuals; in particular, he has regularly taken up the cause of certain Irish prisoners in British jails. But the tenor of his pastoral letter at the end of 1980 established his position on the principle:

> A hunger strike – especially with the threat of continuing until death – is itself a form of violence,

> violence to the hunger-strikers themselves. We must pray, therefore, that the hunger-strikers call off their action.

Latin America was the scene of one of the Cardinal's most specifically successful interventions. In assessing cause and effect in political decision-making it is rare to come across conclusive evidence of why something happened, but Basil Hume provides one such example. In early 1978 he devoted considerable effort to persuading the Labour government to stop selling arms to El Salvador. In February the sales were actually stopped, and Dr David Owen, then the Foreign Secretary, has subsequently disclosed that the Cardinal's appeal was what had swung the decision.

This episode illustrates two enduring aspects of the Hume style in public affairs. First, the arms embargo was achieved by private persuasion rather than public declamation. This is plainly his preferred way of operating. As far as Ministers are concerned, he has been a far more frequent leader of deputations than a denouncer, or even a persuader, from soapbox or pulpit. The method suits his temperament and accords with the mores of Whitehall, and in the case of El Salvador it worked with great effect. Secondly, this particular initiative was undertaken at the request of a brother bishop, Monsignor Oscar Romero, Archbishop of San Salvador, who was later to be murdered in his own cathedral. As Cardinal, Hume has been a true embodiment of the universality of the Church, in the sense that he is swiftest to express practical and verbal solidarity when appeals are made from other branches of the organization, whether in Poland or South Africa or Chile. Bishops in all those countries have had reason to be grateful for his support on matters of human rights and political justice. Although Spanish is not one of his main languages Western-hemisphere Catholicism seems to have supplied one of his more effective communications networks.

With another set of issues, famine and overseas aid, the story has been significantly different. For churchmen, starvation and the unequal distribution of the world's resources have always aroused an uncomplicated response, and this has remained true throughout the 1980s. Church leaders of all denominations have been relatively untouched by the tide of intellectual fashion in this period which has done its best to drown aid programmes in derision and despair. This made aid 'controversial', but churchmen continued to preach against North-South inequities, and Hume has been no exception. Indeed he has gone further than most. As the full horror of the famine in Ethiopia and the Sudan became apparent in 1984, he threw his normal caution overboard and denounced British policy as 'a scandal'. It was one occasion when his generous heart allowed itself to brush aside the more Delphic utterances for which his advisors have a natural taste. Having visited the stricken areas, he returned with new iron in his soul for the governments of the industrialized world which had failed to get the measure of the crisis. There was nothing cloudy in his message, nor any doubt about the link between what God decreed and what man should undertake. From the outside, one had the sense of a man whose eyes had been most horribly opened to the lives of the truly destitute, and who was able to communicate the experience he had undergone. Maybe his words did not raise as much money as Bob Geldof and the Live Aid Concert in July 1985. But they carried more conviction than those of any politician.

If aid has been the issue with least ambiguity, the nuclear question has been much the most agonizing. It occupies a substantial part of the corpus of the Cardinal's public statements. This has been partly by choice – he has thought hard and painfully about war and peace. But partly it was brought about by events: especially by the prominence of one of his priests, Monsignor Bruce Kent, as General

Secretary of the Campaign for Nuclear Disarmament from 1980 to 1985.

Hume plunged into these questions early in his time at Westminster. Arms sales, the global cost of defence expenditures and the moral dilemmas posed by nuclear deterrence itself induced from him a fair number of public declarations. To read them now is to follow a spiritual leader on a difficult personal odyssey. He has always been deeply and sincerely distressed by the world's commitment to its military budgets. 'It is a strange logic', he wrote in 1980, 'which justifies vast expenditure on weapons of destruction while tolerating, according to one estimate, that 800 million people should live in a state of absolute poverty.'

At that time, too, he took an inconclusive line on the nuclear question, writing at the end of the International Year of the Child:

> It is important that we do not lose our sense of reality about the possibility of a nuclear holocaust. The threat of extinction may not seem as urgent and terrifying as it was in the years immediately after the Second World War. Yet today the proliferation of nuclear weapons is a nightmare. Our commitment to the nuclear deterrent creates the immediate possibility of a conflict with the consistent Christian teaching about the right of the innocent to live.

He went on to recall that the Second Vatican Council had declared the indiscriminate destruction of cities and people to be 'a crime against God and man', and then asked:

> If it is wrong to unleash such weapons against civilian targets, can it be morally defensible to threaten to do so even against an unjust oppressor? Can we, in fact, base our defence policy on such threats?

In 1980 he posed these questions without answering them. Three years later he seemed to have resolved some of his doubts. By then they had become a hot political issue. The Campaign for Nuclear Disarmament was at its height. It was entirely characteristic that Hume should resist the pressure from many sources in and out of the Church – including an intemperate and simple-minded attack by the Apostolic Delegate, Archbishop Bruno Heim – to force Mgr Kent to resign his post with CND. In his sensitivity to individual rights and conscience, the Cardinal has been an exemplary superior. But he also worked out a statement affirming his belief in nuclear deterrence and justifying the morality of possessing nuclear weapons. Addressing himself to the nuclear protesters then active at American bases and elsewhere, he added that they did not have the right – 'seriously to break the law'.

This statement was hedged about with caveats. But there is no doubt that, coming when it did, it was helpful to the Government: an accidental rather than an intrinsic effect, but an effect all the same. For the Cardinal personally, it also testified to a diplomatic skill considerably enhanced by seven years in the job. He managed to push it through a Bishops' Conference which was more than usually divided on the subject. In Basil Hume's curriculum vitae as a national as well as an ecclesiastical figure, this merits an entry in bold letters. Nuclear policy is the one centrally controversial issue in British domestic politics where he has chosen to take a prominent and repeated part in the debate.

This is not to say that he has been inactive elsewhere. A variety of social ills, from bad housing to racial discrimination, have received his attention. On such matters he remains uncontaminated by the languor, or even the indifference, which can afflict long-serving princes of the Church. He has also been much more alert than his predecessors when the big moral questions have loomed into everyday politics. An instructive contrast may be drawn between the hesitant Catholic response to the abortion legislation in the 1960s, and the decisive, well-organized opposition to the Warnock report on embryonic experiments in the 1980s. But these, for the Church, are in a sense easy issues. There could be no doubt where it would stand. Of issues in the other, trickier category, only the nuclear dilemma has drawn the Cardinal far into the open.

The fact is that he has chosen restraint as a way of public life. He does not enjoy controversy. One of the best defined prejudices with which he arrived at Westminster was directed against those bishops, mostly Anglican, who sounded off on any issue at the smallest provocation. He has been true to this prejudice in his own conduct. He has become a major national figure while playing a highly selective part in the great national questions, and then rarely giving a lead which could be termed either challenging or abrasive. He is a leader, but one who leads less by what he says than by what he is. Perhaps it is the very fact that this holy and charismatic man says so little about the world, which invests what he stands for with so much relevance to such a wide range of citizens.

There is a paradox here, and in trying to disentangle it, different people will find different threads to lead them through the Hume decade.

One reason, some would say, why he has made his mark closer to the centre of national life than his predecessors is because he fits so snugly into it. For a start, his lack of Irishness is important. Despite his continental origins, he remains the very model of the well-educated middle-class Englishman, with the institutional biases to be expected of one who has spent thirty-five years in a public school, albeit one which was also a Benedictine monastery. The public school network, these critics suggest, is his milieu, and the pleasing rather than the prophetic role his metier. On this analysis, he, and with him the Church, has been accepted into the mainstream of the nation – even, God forbid, into the Establishment – at the price of rarely offending against its canons. If part of the task of the Christian pastor, particularly the Catholic priest, is to act as an irritant to the body politic and an upsetter of its manifold complacencies, Basil Hume is not the man to perform it.

He himself would powerfully reject this. Socially he may be a conservative, as he is theologically a liberal. But no one so wholly unambitious for power or position fits naturally into the political establishment, and nobody so naturally at home with the meek of the earth can be other than unsettling to those who are not meek at all. As evidence for this, one need look no further than his encounter with the Prime Minister on his return from Ethiopia, by all accounts a frosty meeting with a politician recently unenthused by interfering bishops and carrying the anti-Catholic baggage of a lifetime. Basil Hume is still a northerner and still a monk, and his years in the metropolis have not failed to leave him somewhat cynical about metropolitan power and how it is operated. If he has joined the Establishment, it is partly by courtesy and partly by accident, not with malice aforethought: drawn into governing or royal circles because he is such a palpably wise and sympathetic man, with whom the great as well as the small are happy to entrust their confidences.

There is, in any case, another dimension to the empathy he attracts. His salient characteristics, unvarnished and uninvented, are an appealing antidote to the times in which he has become a famous man.

If he has been wary of controversy, it is partly because he believes there are other things to talk about more pertinent to this mortal life than industrial relations or the Gross National Product. Not only more pertinent but better suited to the priestly vocabulary he understands. Quite early in his tenure, when launching an organization called Christians for Social Justice, he did make a specific appeal for Catholics to involve themselves more actively in social and political affairs. On another occasion at about the same time, he vowed publicly to be more outspoken about the welfare of society, and urged his priests to be the same. But he has not lived up to this aspiration to the extent he seemed to be promising.

Instead he has done something else. He has sought to point the nation towards a more spiritual life, in language he makes more intelligible and real than any other Church leader in the English-speaking world. To a society soaked in materialism he offers the richer vision of poverty and self-abnegation: a vision which, with one part of its being, it still wishes to hear about. To a society supposedly turning away from God, the Cardinal supplies images of the godly life which give modern coherence to a timeless idea.

Nor is that the most seductive challenge he makes to the prevailing style. In an age of certainties, he is the original doubting Thomas. Modern politicians seek, and sometimes claim to have found, a series of categoric imperatives. The 1980s have been dominated by their absolute convictions, and their belief that it was hesitation and doubt which, more than anything, had undone the governments of the recent past. Although this adamant approach was popular for a time, because it purported to banish failure and promise success, it was out of harmony with the English pragmatic tradition. By his very diffidence, and the resolute sparseness of his worldly assertions, Father Basil has spoken well to that tradition. At a time when dogma reigned in the secular world, the undogmatic Cardinal became a figure held in particular esteem.

This style has meant that he has left things unsaid and tasks not done. He does not enjoy executive power, and he does not like making decisive judgements. A tendency to vacillate goes hand in hand with a deeply ingrained preference for kindness and toleration. His emphasis on the spiritual, together with his reluctance to interpret spirituality in the terms of a prophetic political message, may sometimes be disappointing to Catholics who seek more direct engagement with modern issues. As leader of the European as well as the national bishops, he is one of the most powerful churchmen in the world – but one with large reserves of his moral authority unexpended. Some people find this very frustrating.

He has none the less made spirituality real. He lifts our eyes to a far horizon. Both to Catholics and in the world beyond any church, that perhaps constitutes Basil Hume's uniqueness.